Urban High School Students and the Challenge of Access

"*Urban High School Students and the Challenge of Access* is a powerful and poignant year-long account of the lives of high school graduates in a working-class neighborhood of Los Angeles. Charting the different post-graduation pathways of five of these students, the authors present gripping and illuminating accounts of the complex dynamics among high school, college, and urban life and the perils and promises that are in store for many young people today. Every student reacts to the brute inequalities of modern life differently, and the authors powerfully capture these differences and offer major steps that educational institutions can take to improve substantially their chances of success. This is an important book!

> Peter McLaren, *Graduate School of Education and Information Studies,*
> *University of California, Los Angeles; Author of*
> Capitalists and Conquerors: A Critical Pedagogy Against Empire

"This is an engaging book that paints the picture behind the numbers. Through the use of cultural biography, the authors take us into the lives of low-income students struggling to become college-goers in spite of enormous handicaps. This is a hopeful text, one that shatters stereotypes about low-income students, and examines how some students who shouldn't make it to college, do. We can learn a great deal from this wonderful book about how to shape policy with real kids—not just numbers—in mind."

> Patricia Gándara, *Professor, University of California, Davis*

"This book focuses on the greatest challenge facing higher education—the inaccessibility of colleges for the poor and minorities. This book stands out: The research is powerful and the conclusions are compelling and practical."

> Arthur Levine, *President, Teachers College, Columbia University*

"As debates continue to rage over the quality of urban education, this outstanding volume gives voice to the very students at the center of these virtual struggles for educational access and success. Cultural biographies reveal the complexity of adolescent lived experiences embedded in neighborhood social contexts. We see how these remarkable students negotiate the often-treacherous pathways to college and beyond. Clear lessons emerge for educational practice and policy in urban schooling from this tour de force study."

> Walter R. Allen, *Allan Murray Cartter Professor of Higher Education*
> *and Professor of Sociology, Graduate School of Education*
> *and Information Studies, University of California, Los Angeles*

Urban High School Students and the Challenge of Access

Questions about the Purpose(s) of Colleges & Universities

Norm Denzin, Joe L. Kincheloe, Shirley R. Steinberg
General Editors

Vol. 17

PETER LANG
New York • Washington, D.C./Baltimore • Bern
Frankfurt am Main • Berlin • Brussels • Vienna • Oxford

Urban High School Students and the Challenge of Access

MANY ROUTES, DIFFICULT PATHS

William G. Tierney & Julia E. Colyar,
EDITORS

PETER LANG
New York • Washington, D.C./Baltimore • Bern
Frankfurt am Main • Berlin • Brussels • Vienna • Oxford

Library of Congress Cataloging-in-Publication Data

Urban high school students and the challenge of access:
many routes, difficult paths /
edited by William G. Tierney & Julia E. Colyar.
p. cm. — (Higher ed: questions about the purpose(s)
of colleges and universities; v. 17)
Includes bibliographical references and index.
1. Youth with social disabilities—Education (Higher)—United States. 2. Urban youth—Education
(Higher)—United States. 3. Educational equalization—United States.
I. Tierney, William G. II. Colyar, Julia E. III. Series: Higher ed; v. 17.
LC4091.U735   378.1'9826'9420973—dc22   2005022539
ISBN 0-8204-6326-4
ISSN 1523-9551

Bibliographic information published by **Die Deutsche Bibliothek**.
Die Deutsche Bibliothek lists this publication in the "Deutsche
Nationalbibliografie"; detailed bibliographic data is available
on the Internet at http://dnb.ddb.de/.

Cover design by Lisa Barfield

The paper in this book meets the guidelines for permanence and durability
of the Committee on Production Guidelines for Book Longevity
of the Council of Library Resources.

Contents

...

Acknowledgments

...

We are grateful to Norm Denzin, Yvonna Lincoln, Shirley Steinberg, and Joe Kincheloe for their review and support of this manuscript, and we appreciate the assistance of Christopher Myers in all the stages of editing and production. Several friends and colleagues also reviewed early drafts of the chapters, and we are thankful for their careful readings.

For their unfailing support, we are indebted to Monica Raad and Diane Flores at the Center for Higher Education Policy Analysis (CHEPA) at the University of Southern California. Their administrative assistance made this project—and all of our work—much easier.

We are also thankful for the assistance of college preparation program staff, administrators, teachers, and students at the schools we visited. Their experiences and insights informed our understandings of students and college access. We appreciate their willingness to open their offices and classrooms for scrutiny.

Without the students and families presented in these pages, this project would not have been possible. Their time, energy, and trust were invaluable. We hope that these chapters convey our deep admiration for their hard work, intelligence, commitment, and imagination. Yeni, Trinity, Juan, Mushutu, and Lily, we thank you and look forward to learning about your continued success.

Royalties from this book will be donated to the American Indian College Fund and the Mexican American Legal Defense and Educational Fund.

1

•• ••• ••• •••

William G. Tierney

Introduction

SÍ, SE PUEDE

•••

The day arrives with what Angelinos have come to label, "June gloom"—a thick layer of marine fog lies heavily over the city—but it is hardly gloomy for the students with whom we have spent the past 12 months. Today is high school graduation for most of them. Juan awakens early and puts in a call to his father to make sure he will drive him to graduation. Even though his father is not going to attend the ceremony, he has offered to take his son to school so that his green cap and gown won't get dirty. Trinity calls to find out how to put on the gown. "I think I have a white collar thing. How does it go? Do I have to wear all my medals?" she asks. "Where does the tassel go on the hat? On the left or right?" Lily figures out a way for her two older sisters to attend graduation. "The four tickets we were allowed just wasn't going to cut it," she laughs, but with a sense of urgency, "my sisters would've died if they couldn't see me graduate." Across town, Mushutu, having just found out he got straight A's again for his junior year, enrolls in a summer program for accounting. "Accounting, it's boring," he relates. "But I couldn't find anything else. It's like a refresher for my math skills. I can't let them get rusty." Up the coast, Jenny graduated from high school a week ago. She finally has time to sleep in and spend time with her brothers and sister.

Our challenge has been to examine the different pathways that brought these students to where they are today; their stories provide clues about how to improve college access at urban high schools. In the ensuing chapters, the portraits of five remarkable students and the contexts in which they are embedded emerge. As we discuss in the Afterword, we have utilized a methodology that demanded an intense engagement between the students, their families and friends, their teachers and ourselves. We met with each of these students every week for over a year. We sat in their classes, watched night football games, had meals with their parents, went to homecomings and proms, and attended their churches. We were sounding boards for the students on the many personal issues that punctuate adolescent life, and we advised them about what college will be like.

By situating ourselves in these texts and moving the students to center stage we are calling upon a different strategy from those methodological tactics that are currently in vogue. All too often discussions about the problems of high schools and the challenge of access to college overlooks the very individuals about whom there is so much purported concern—the students themselves. The challenge of access to higher education in twenty-first-century America is not a blur of images void of faces and personalities. Although we do not quarrel with much of the fine analytical work that seeks to summarize educational strengths and weaknesses on a meta-scale, we remain convinced that if change is going to happen, then a commitment to, and recognition of, individuals must remain at the forefront of educational policy-related research. Otherwise, educational change becomes little more than a political chess match where the students end up as pawns. Individual life stories highlight the urgency of the changes that are necessary. It is difficult to forget that without sufficient financial aid, Mushutu's straight A's will be irrelevant and Jenny won't be the first in her family to earn an undergraduate degree.

Thus, in the chapters that follow we document a year in the life of adolescents who are trying to figure out not simply where they want to go to college, or what they want to do when they graduate from high school, but who they want to be. Our intent in focusing on these lives is not simply to present cheery portraits of students who are working hard and who might actually make it, but instead to highlight the inequities that circumscribe their daily existence. Living in poverty, attending overcrowded schools, and the pressure to be the first in their families to attend college are just a few of the challenges these students face en route to college. Indeed, these challenges also impact their chances of persistence once there. We tie these biographies together in the conclusion by suggesting what they mean for practice and policy. We are not arguing that these portraits are the equivalent of the educational world in a teacup. However, we suggest that an educational treatise void of any sense of engagement with students and their families is methodologically and civically flawed. The conclusion, then, ties these stories together and presents them within today's broader educational currents. From these stories and their contexts we develop strategies for improving the educational opportunities of these students and their friends. The goal is for the reader to gain a sense of the excitement and pride these students and their families feel today as they graduate from high school, and to consider how that journey might be improved for the students who follow them into high school and across the graduation stage.

By five o'clock in the afternoon the neighborhood surrounding the school is packed with cars. "It's like a football night," says one student. Rosa's Food truck is parked near the gym and Rosa is doing a brisk business; corn dogs on a stick are selling particularly well. A handful of vendors walk the streets holding baskets with Cheetos and chips and do a good business with the multitude of children milling around waiting for their older brothers and sisters "to get graduated" as one young boy says. Roses and balloons are the best sellers; fathers and boyfriends buy out one vendor's stock. The woman calls to her husband to get more flowers from the back of their old station wagon. A man selling stuffed animals sits disconsolately on the low wall outside the high school offering discounts as the time gets closer to the ceremony. Moments later, a police car pulls up to the school's gate and announces over the loudspeaker: "You do not have a permit to sell things. Leave or you will be cited." Vendors frantically pack their remaining items and wheel carts down the street.

"Let's go, seniors. Hurry up. We need you downstairs. We start walking in 15 minutes," emanates from Mr. Jones's bullhorn. The seniors have chosen dark green as their class color and a sea of green begins to assemble on the far side of the gym. Juan runs by in a gown that barely covers his knees but nevertheless cost $50 to buy. "It's expensive, yes," he had reflected earlier, "but I'm graduating. Of course I'll pay the money." The class salutatorian, Michael, saunters by, easily a head taller than everyone else and calls out: "Yo, Enrique. Wait for me. We'll walk together." The omnipresent cell phones seem glued to every other student's ear as they enter the alleyway and line up to march.

"All students should be inside. If you're not inside in five minutes you're going to miss out on graduation. C'mon. Hurry up. Now! Move it, seniors!"

Graduation is on the football field and the stands are already full with parents, family, friends, and brothers and sisters. A long line awaits people as they try to get through the gates to their seats. "I don't care if you just bought them," says one attendant, "It's school policy. You can't take balloons in. You have to check them." Another usher reiterates, "No robillos inside." Because graduates have a limit of four tickets each, some students madly scramble to find extras for more family members. It seems as if as many people are standing outside the gates overlooking the stadium and on the streets around it as there are families inside in the stands.

The high school band is making a spirited attempt at entertaining the crowd, but they end up slightly off key; some of the seniors in the band race away when they see everyone lined up so that they can walk with their friends. The band strikes up a ragged "Pomp and Circumstance" and the seniors begin to walk. They enter under a huge arch of green balloons with the word "Luminaries" inscribed. After Mr. Satterfield, the husband of the school's volleyball coach, sings the national anthem, the principal gets up to welcome everyone. He speaks of the pride that the students and their families and friends should feel in getting to this momentous day. Of 577 students, 33 will be attending a University of California campus and another 35 will attend a state college. Over half of them will go to a community college, and the rest will most likely try to find work in Los Angeles. He is proud of this year's graduates, he tells the crowd, despite the fact that he wishes there were more of them. Throughout the two-hour event various speakers point out how important graduation is, but that it is only a start to the graduate's adult life. Many speakers depict graduation as a community event made possible by multiple individuals who have pitched in to help the seniors.

The student organizers and the speakers give their speeches in English and Spanish so that the parents of the graduates might understand what is being said. As is often true for graduations, there is a sense of excitement and lightheartedness that makes it difficult for students to concentrate. At one point, a modified wave breaks out. The valedictorian gets up to give her address and begins by singing, a capella, "Amazing grace, how sweet the sound that saved a wretch like me. . . ." She gives a moving speech expressing her gratitude for all of the changes she has gone through over her high school years, then finishes, singing, "I once was lost but now I'm found. Was blind but now I see." The salutatorian applauds his teachers: "They are like confidants, like family, they're always here. Some teachers are here at six in the morning; my academy teacher is here until eight at night. I couldn't have gotten here without them." The head of the school board delivers the keynote. "Sí se puede is not just a slogan," he explains. "It's a way of life."

The procession of graduates starts and every student's name is called. Three stages are set up because of the large number of graduates, and as each walks across the makeshift platforms to shake hands and receive their diploma, the graduates' families applaud. Pausing quickly, each student has a photograph taken. A beach ball comes out of nowhere and lifts above the crowd of students, only to disappear almost immediately as a teacher grabs it and carries it away. When the last student receives his diploma the principal returns to the podium and says, "By the power vested in me by the state of California, I hereby declare you the graduates of the class of 2004." Fireworks light up the sky.

The final speaker, a student, returns to the podium and says, "Don't forget where you came from. I love you guys. We need to come back and be involved. Never forget this place or each other. At the count of three turn your tassels from left to right. "One! Two! . . ."

2

... ...

Paz M. Olivérez

Urban Students, Social Ecologies—Part I

...

THE COMMUNITY

The popular image of Los Angeles as a sprawling metropolis where the rich and famous can be spotted driving fancy cars down palm tree-lined boulevards reflects little of the reality of many L.A. residents. In the year 2000, the U.S. Census reported that 22.1% of Los Angeles residents lived below the poverty line—a 46% increase from the 15.1% recorded ten years earlier. The neighborhood surrounding Esperanza High School, where many of the students whose stories will be told here live, is one of the city's most densely populated with over 19,000 residents per square mile. Many families in this downtown L.A. neighborhood work for minimum wage or less and consequently live far below the poverty line. The average family size in this particular section of Los Angeles is 3.65 persons, and the average yearly income is $24,074. According to the 1990 census, Esperanza's residential area had the highest percentage ranking with regard to the number of immigrants, noncitizens, low-income families, second-language households, and persons without high schools diplomas.

In this neighborhood, one can spend hours without hearing a word of English. The community is 60% immigrant: 62% Latino, 3% African American, 16% Asian, and 16% White. The busy streets are saturated with people, cars, apartment buildings, discount stores, locally owned Mexican, Salvadoran, and Korean restaurants, and street vendors selling everything from toys to "tortas" (sandwiches). These details are unmistakable to the casual observer. Less evident are the things missing from this section of the city—privileges that the middle-class and wealthy would never permit their children to go without. There is one library and no bookstores easily accessible to students. If a student who received a 650 combined score on his SAT wants to acquire a study manual before retaking the test, it is unclear where he can go to get one.

Because of the large student-aged population and limited number of schools in the area, the majority of Esperanza students have attended multi-track schools their entire lives; the neighborhood schools are vastly overcrowded. There are two Bank of America branches in this area, but check cashing and cash advance shops occupy space in every strip mall. Despite efforts to make the two large parks in the area more welcoming to residents, most students describe them as unsafe and forbidden places where their parents will not allow them to go. Both parks are viewed as havens for the homeless, drug-pushers and users, and those dealing in false documentation.

The fact that approximately 27% of the inhabitants are undocumented immigrants contributes to a thriving underground economy. Fake identification and social security cards are sold in the park so that locals can obtain jobs in hotels, office buildings, fast food restaurants, and sweat shops. Regardless of their immigration and employment status, though, few earn more than minimum wage. Some make less, and few have health benefits. When one looks around at the hard-working people of this neighborhood—one of L.A.'s poorest—the "hustle" is everywhere. The men and women are of various ages and national origins. Whether it is selling "paletas" (popsicles) on the street corners or cosmetics out of their homes, most struggle daily to survive, never really getting ahead. Few of the residents have ever experienced living in or owning single-family homes, having tree-lined streets, or living in clean, well-kept neighborhoods. These are luxuries that minimum wage and sweat shop pay cannot provide. In fact, 92% of the inhabitants in the area live in an apartment or duplex, and 83% are renters. Many families move frequently, but few move out of the neighborhood altogether. Students report that their families pay rent ranging from $700 to $1,400 to live in what one student described as "inhumane" conditions.

According to the district's demographic experts, almost 10,000 high school-aged students currently live in the area surrounding Esperanza High School. In addition, despite the large number of young people in this neighborhood, the city continues to approve construction of large multi-family dwellings in the immediate area. The number of new students outpaces the space available in the schools by a wide margin. For two decades and ending in the spring of 2004, the school district mandated that students living less than a half a mile southwest of the high school be bussed to a school 18 miles away because of overcrowding.

Many of Esperanza's students walk or take the city bus to school every day. These students may live right down the street or up to three miles away. The latter tend to get dropped off at school by parents who prefer that their girls in particular avoid the sometimes dangerous public transportation system. Students' living situations vary, although most Esperanza students live in one- or two-bedroom apartments with families typically consisting of four or more. Few of these students have ever experienced living in a house, having a yard, a pet, or even a family car. When asked about the luxuries that they believe a college education will afford them, many Esperanza students mention cars, jewelry, and pets. Despite their modest living situations, most Esperanza students do not view themselves as different—everyone they know lives the same way. Even so, when asked, many describe themselves as poor or low-income and view their educational experiences similarly. Esperanza students who wish to attend community college to earn credits toward high school graduation or college must travel at least five miles to get to the closest one, Los Angeles City College. The students who do attend community college typically get there by city bus.

When observing the immediate neighborhood near Esperanza, the viewer quickly becomes aware of the constant activity and abundant poverty. The neighborhood rests in the shadows of downtown's immense wealth and towering skyscrapers. Small dilapidated apartment buildings and homes literally piled on top of each other line the nearby streets that house Esperanza's community of Latino and Southeast Asian immigrant residents. Just beyond these buildings are a Korean church and a small neighborhood school, which serve the students of these two communities. East of the immediate Esperanza neighborhood is downtown Los Angeles, but the downtown area is separated from this community by the 110 freeway overpass, a major roadway stretching from Pasadena to South Los Angeles and beyond. One teacher at Esperanza describes this neighborhood as "the Ellis Island" of Los Angeles, where immigrants come when they first arrive in the city, before they go on to plant roots in other communities farther away from downtown.

THE SCHOOL

Esperanza High School is located in the Los Angeles Unified School District (LAUSD), which consists of 56 high schools and encompasses nearly 704 square miles. Twenty-six cities are partially or entirely within the LAUSD. The district is predominantly Latino (72%), with African Americans making up the next largest group (12%), followed by Whites (9%), and Asians (4%). Of the high schools in the LAUSD, Esperanza is one of the largest with over 5,000 students. The school is one of the two most overcrowded high schools in Los Angeles and one of the ten most populated in the nation. Consequently, the school, its staff, and students face multiple challenges unknown to those at high schools in more affluent parts of the city. Students in Beverly Hills and Palos Verdes do not worry so much about up-to-date textbooks, a desk for every student, and the better quality of education that goes along with them.

Because of its large student population, Esperanza is forced to focus much of its energy and resources on getting students through the school day, the school year, and sometimes into college. The latter is clearly the most difficult, particularly at a school that when compared to others in more affluent areas, sends 50% fewer of its students to 4-year institutions of higher education. In recent years, a debate about academic preparation has been raging in Los Angeles. At one time many inner-city schools such as Esperanza lacked the honors and advanced placement (AP) courses typically credited with preparing students for college. All schools in the district subsequently added such courses. Today, Esperanza offers nearly as many types of AP courses as schools in more affluent areas. Esperanza, however, offers only one or two sections of each subject, and the quality of the courses is often questioned. Because many of Esperanza's students have lacked adequate academic preparation before high school, advanced placement courses must often be "dumbed down" to meet these students' needs, forcing those better prepared students to lag behind with their less prepared classmates. As the subsequent chapters will show, such circumstances are common for high-achieving students at many overcrowded urban high schools.

During the 2002–2003 school year, 50% of Esperanza's AP students completed AP exams. A similar percentage of students at City View High School, a local public high school in an affluent neighborhood, also completed AP exams. But the disparity in student performance is telling: During the 2002–2003 school year, only 13% of the 313 AP students at Esperanza who took AP exams received a passing score. At City View, 437 students took AP exams and 75% received a passing score. If these scores offer any indication, Esperanza seems to be doing a rather poor job preparing its students for college.

The disparity in academic performance is probably the consequence of a variety of factors. City View has a student population less than half the size of Esperanza's and is nearly 75% white; the school operates on a traditional nine-month schedule; and only 6% of City View's students are eligible for the free/reduced lunch program. Eighty percent of Esperanza's students participate in the free/reduced lunch program, and almost all are non-white. AP course offerings are so limited at Esperanza High School that some of them have 50 students enrolled or more, while few, if any, of the classes at City

View have even 30 students. Perhaps even more importantly, students at Esperanza do not receive the individualized college counseling afforded to all of City View's students.

As a result of its desire to implement the practices of higher-performing school districts, Esperanza's governing "mini-district" recently mandated that all students complete first-year algebra in order to graduate. In this way, the mini-district demonstrates a commitment to college preparation. Despite these somewhat noble intentions, however, the practice has been disastrous for Esperanza's incoming students, many of whom are several math levels below algebra upon entering high school. Over 60% of Esperanza's students fail the class, and many will go on to repeat it several times. Students and administrators report that the new algebra requirement can be blamed for the ever-increasing number of Esperanza students who drop out of high school. "These one-size-fits-all edicts ask our students to perform at the same level as students across the district when they haven't received the same level of preparation. If this were medicine it would be called malpractice," explained Mr. Mason, Esperanza's head counselor.

3

• • • • • • • • • • • •

William G. Tierney

Mushutu and Juan

A TALE OF TWO STUDENTS

• • •

MUSHUTU'S WORLD

"Are you the substitute for English or physics?" the vice principal inquires. When I say "neither," that I am here to observe a student who is in Mr. Vasquez's first-period English class and need directions, he shrugs his shoulders. "Go out the doors here, turn left, walk across the quad, there's a building perpendicular from Doolittle, the Art building. It's in there. I think it's on the second floor." He turns away from me and back to the flood of students who need attention.

As I go out into the quad and make my way to the classroom, I am momentarily stunned. Students are everywhere. Overcrowding has hit Los Angeles schools, and classroom size has inched back up to 1980 levels. I keep walking, try to remember what perpendicular means, find a building, and start walking up the flight of stairs.

"Professor, professor," I hear behind me as I reach the top of the stairs. I turn to see Mushutu running after me. "This is the wrong building. You walked right by the building; I saw you. Come this way," he beckons. We turn and retrace my steps.

Mushutu is 17, an exceptionally good student who is highly motivated, and extremely polite. When he received a 1380 on his SATs a few weeks ago, he was disappointed because he wanted a 1400. When he got his score he sent me an email: "How are you? I am doing ok, but I have to start with the bad news. It seems as if I am jinxed. My cumulative SAT score is 1380. All is lost! I know you wanted me to get a 1450, but I hoped that if I at least got a 1400 I could go to a good college. I must study harder."

It will be difficult for Mushutu to study any harder than he already does. He takes three APs: English, chemistry, and history. He also participates in the Model United Nations, chess club, teen jury, MESA (Math, Engineering, Science Achievement), academic decathlon, two college preparation programs in the summer, debate club, academy of finance, and Junior Leaders of America. I speak with him once a week on Friday afternoons at 4:30; it is the only time he can fit me into his busy schedule.

Mushutu is wearing sandals, white socks, khakis, a thin green t-shirt, a bracelet his auntie presented to him, and a cross that hangs around his neck. "I don't think I'm very religious, no," he says, when I ask about the cross. "But when my mother left Ethiopia to come here she gave it to me, and I have kept it on ever since. I never take it off." He has light black skin, short wiry hair, and just the hint of a mustache; he doesn't realize it yet, but he's going to be handsome. He has deep, expressive eyes and he speaks rapidly in great gulps of paragraphs with his left hand frequently punctuating the air to help him make his point.

"O no," he says. "I don't go out on dates. I need to stay focused on my goals. Girls can make you lose sight of your goals." Over the course of the year I tease him from time to time about why he doesn't go out and have fun, and he always maintains a similar response. "Someday I will, but not now. I have too much homeworks, too much to do to get into college." He also finds himself at events that he considers "too sexual." He went away on a class trip for a model United Nations to a neighboring city where the students stayed in a hotel overnight and some of the girls and boys apparently made out with one another. "It was very interesting during the day, very fun. But then it was so strange at night. Gosh, things got so sexual. I went back to my room; I had a history paper to write." When Janet Jackson's "wardrobe malfunction" happened at the Super Bowl, Mushutu thought it was emblematic of America: "It was inappropriate, I would say. To do that in front of all those people. I don't think you should act that way."

Even male friends are pretty much out of the question. "I'm casual. I'll say hello and everything, but not friends like you mean, like go to the movies or hang out or just play after school. I don't have time for that. It can distract you. I don't want to waste my life." One day an older student whom Mushutu knows but whom he hasn't seen for a while comes up to him, and they go through a ritual handshake; Mushutu stands with his hands on his hips and speaks with the high school senior for a few minutes before they separate. The senior says to me, "He's a nice guy. Real hard-working. He's the kind of guy people won't mess with. He knows his way around."

Although he likes America, he still does not entirely understand the mores of his classmates. "Like Goth," he says one day, shaking his head back and forth, "what's that about? I don't get it." At Halloween he tells me he wants nothing to do with it and has made sure his little brother doesn't go out. "He's sort of mad at me, I would say, because he wants candies. But I think it's creepy. It's like a satanic cult. There are people running around putting blood on, and masks and all that creepy stuff. It's also very commercial. I just stay away from things like that."

When we reach his classroom, Mr. Vasquez hasn't arrived yet, and the door is still locked. We stand to a side by ourselves and talk. "I arrive here early every day. It's easier." He motions to the quad. "There's so much noise, so many kids. I get here and do my homeworks, or review what I completed last night, yeah." A few of his classmates are standing off to the side, and he neither says hello nor do they appear to note his or my existence. I ask him if there are areas of school that he avoids. "Like gangs?" he asks. He points over toward the track. "I stay away from there, or behind that building. That's where kids do drugs." He points to a distant building that borders a side street. "When I first came here I was a little afraid, it was a little scary, but I like it now. I know my way around. I just wish people took their classes more seriously."

One theme we return to throughout our conversations is Mushutu's relationship with people and his reliance on himself. One day I give him a sheet with words on it such as "family, church, school, teachers, myself" and ask him to circle the words that are likely to help him get into college. He circles only one: "myself." "You have to rely on yourself," he tells me. "It's not like people are bad or anything, but if you're going to do it, if you're going to succeed, then you have to make it." I ask him another day who his role models are and he immediately says, "I don't want role models. I need to create my own principles and ideas."

Even his family seem tangential to him. His mother emigrated from Ethiopia to get away from political repression, and she wanted to raise her daughter and two sons in the United States. She moved to Los Angeles because she had relatives here; she lived alone for two years until the family had enough money for Mushutu, his younger brother, and older sister to emigrate. Last year his father arrived. "Well, I love them, yes," he tells me, "and of course I do what they tell me to do, but they don't really know about college, about what I do at school. We came here to America because I was always sort of an American kid. Not flashy, like some kids, but wanting to learn, wanting to succeed."

When he first arrived in Los Angeles, his family lived in one of the poorest sections of the city known as "the Jungle." The violence and poverty that surrounded him in the Jungle surprised him. In an essay he writes for a fellowship, "I thought America was a land of riches and pleasures because of what I had seen in the movies. It proved to be the opposite. The Jungle is a neighborhood where if I make a wrong turn a bullet will whistle towards my head. I have had a continuous fear that I would one day be a victim of violence." At the end of this essay Mushutu returns to his theme of self-hood:

> Poverty has not stopped me. I want to change the world. Not only do I want to see a decrease in violence, but I also want to learn as much as I can so that I can help others. In order for me to succeed, I will not have the benefits of rich kids who go to good schools and have private tutors. I only have one weapon: a desire to learn. I work very hard; I study every night and on the weekend. I am determined to improve the world by showing that there are people who are willing to make a difference and willing to be an example for others. America is not a land of riches for those of us who live in the Jungle, but it can be a land of opportunities for everyone: success is up to me.

JUAN'S WORLD

A few weeks before I visit Mushutu's class I spend the day with Juan; he is a Mexican immigrant who came over the border with his mother when he was five. "A coyote guided us. I don't remember much. Just lots of walking. My father, he was here already."

Juan lives in a one-room apartment near MacArthur Park in Los Angeles with his mom and younger brother, Diego. Unlike Mushutu who is voluble and animated every time I speak with him, Juan is quiet and reserved. He tends to answer questions in monosyllables, and I need to prod him to expand on his ideas. Part of his reticence is that he has not spoken to anyone about his life. Week by week he begins to tell of different parts of growing up in L.A. He initially speaks of his family, and continually returns to this theme during our time together:

> My father moved out two years ago. It's good he left. When we first moved here I got used to my dad. He would take us places, like a trip, not far, but just to have some fun. And that's basically stuff I used to do with my dad and play soccer.

> It was tough when he left, because it really hurts when someone just leaves, but then you think back and you begin to understand the situation from before and how my dad used to hit my mom, and in a way it's good he left. They always fought, they would argue, and then he would say 'I am sorry' but then it begins again. He has a girlfriend now. I don't think that's right.

I'm not angry at my dad. I'm a calm person. I basically don't hate him, maybe there are reasons to hate, but I just see him for what he is. He used to hit me lots of times. One good kick to make me understand, or to answer something. He started to hit me when I was young. Since I was the oldest he hit me more because I was the oldest boy; he didn't hit Diego very much. I never knew why he hit me so much; I wasn't terrible.

Juan worries that his younger brother is going to be violent like his father. "He has problems in school. He's in seventh grade and gets in trouble a lot. Me, I'm calm like my mother, in a way, but Diego is like my father and it's hard to control him."

Juan loves his mother and respects how hard she works. She is on a janitorial staff at a McDonald's across the city and works from 4 A.M. until noon. In order to get to work on time she gets up at 2 A.M. to catch a series of buses. During the bus strike in Los Angeles it took her even longer. She is in a catch-22; the McDonald's is in a nice area of Los Angeles where she could never afford to live, but they will hire her because she is undocumented. She receives cash for her work and she is able to make ends meet, but she could never afford a car. She also could not get a legal driver's license, and has neither a checking account nor a credit card. "We hide the monies in our house," Juan smiles, "sometimes we forget where we put it."

Juan eventually tells me that he also works. His father got him a job working on the janitorial staff of a downtown hotel. Because he also is undocumented, he has used Diego's social security card—Diego was born in the United States—and is able to get a paycheck. He works 24 hours a week—one day after school from four until midnight, and Saturday and Sunday evenings. He is the only teenager on an all-Latino crew of workers. "At first I was surprised, but it's better that they are adult. They are more serious."

He works to help his mother pay the rent and put food on the table. The greatest extravagance he has spent on himself is when he bought a computer—"from a guy on the street"—about a year ago so that he could use the Internet and the Web to search for colleges and financial aid. He buys his own clothes and usually wears a plain blue shirt with a t-shirt underneath and a pair of tan khaki pants. He wears heavy black shoes and occasionally uses thin black glasses. He is 5 foot 4 and weighs about 130 pounds. Over the last year he has been trying to grow a mustache, but otherwise he keeps himself conservatively groomed and neatly dressed. He wears a gold chain around his neck that his mom gave him a long time ago. He never takes it off. His buzz cut accentuates that his ears stick out. He has deep brown eyes and a pleasant smile when he is willing to use it, but the defining characteristic for Juan is his shyness, what he calls "being calm."

"My English, it's not good, I know," he explains in a characteristically quiet voice. "I'm not speaking in class very much because it's just not good. I don't want to be humiliated so I try to ignore others." His teachers know who he is, but because he is neither an excellent student nor a problem, he has been able to float through his high school years without developing any lasting relationships with any teachers. One teacher explains to me, "Juan is very quiet, reserved. He just sort of comes into class and sits there. He's late a lot too, but it's not acting out. I think he's the type of kid who counselors move around like chess pieces, putting them in classes where there's space. I never knew him before he got placed in here." He had been sent to an AP class in the second semester of his senior year because the counselor suddenly recognized Juan needed a class like that in order to meet graduation requirements. Juan had never been in an honors or AP class before but he was placed in the AP class because there was space. He ended up with a D, but he would graduate.

Juan enters and leaves his classes by himself. He always sits toward the front of the room and writes in his diligently kept notebook throughout the class. Other students sit in groups of two or three and casually chat amongst themselves, but Juan keeps to himself. "I have some friends," he states, "Mamadu is African, and we talk politics a lot, and Sergio and I sometimes talk, but I'm calm, not so much into the social activities. I don't really know how to have fun, in a way. I just go on my own." He used to play soccer on weekends, but he has given that up as well because he needs to work.

He has never been to a dance, to homecoming, or even taken a girl on a date. Girls are a mystery. "I don't know what to say. I couldn't speak to them. I get nervous." When I suggest that he should invite someone to a spring dance he laughs in a way that makes it clear that I could just as well have suggested he sprout wings and fly. "What if the girl, she knows how to dance better than me? I'd be too embarrassed."

He says about himself: "A few call me 'dumbo' because of my ears, but I just ignore them. Calling names is stupid. They don't hurt me; I forgive them. I'm not interested in what they like. I'm also not a handsome guy, like Pedro. He always has a girlfriend, and he jokes with me that he could get me someone, but I don't want it like that. It's not right." Juan says he enjoys his time by himself, or rather, "It's just what I do. You always ask if I'm happy and I don't know what is that, but sad? I guess sometimes I might be sad, like sometimes I wish I could speak to a girl, but I just live my life in a calm way."

Unlike Mushutu, who seems to schedule his time like a frenetic executive, Juan always has time to see me. He was in JROTC for two years, but he came to realize that he wouldn't be able to join the military because he was undocumented; given the problems in the world, he also decided being a soldier was not very attractive. He has participated in MESA, but finds it "not very interesting." Other than school work and his job, he does not participate in many formal or informal activities. "I do not go to MacArthur Park," he relates "It's dangerous there, in certain parts, people sell drugs." He goes to mass on most Sundays with his mother, and in the final term of his school year he starts taking a public speaking class at a community college. "Maybe if I take the class my English improves and I won't be nervous," he explains. The class meets on Friday evenings and he has to take a bus for about an hour to reach the community college. Because he works on Saturday nights, Juan has no free time for social activities on weekends. "In a sense, I like it that way," he explains. "It keeps me busy."

"I want a college degree to better myself," Juan states, but the entire college process is a mystery. "I think I want to be a paralegal," he says one day, and later he decides he wants to get into computers, and still later, perhaps a paramedic. At one point he brings in a book by Hegel that he has gotten from the library and thinks he might like to study history, "it's very interesting." At another time he has the writings of St. Augustine; he finds the book "very difficult, but some of the sentences, they are good for me to understand." He has never spoken to a college counselor for an extended period of time, but he does use the computer in the high school's college room.

When I ask Juan about the costs of college he knows the precise dollar amounts for different institutions and recognizes that he will have to get financial aid if he goes anywhere other than a community college. "But a four-year degree, that's better," he says. "You need a four-year degree for a professional job." He has gotten a 660 on the SAT, has a 2.0 GPA and has flunked sophomore year, so his chances of getting into a public institution are slim. He also doesn't have the profile of someone for whom a private institution would find a scholarship because of his low GPA and SAT scores.

He uses the Web extensively to search for information about college and how to pay for it. At one point he and I are searching different financial aid Web sites, and we come upon one that he has used in the past. "I'm already on this Web," he informs me. "What's your log-on," I ask? "John," he says, "John Flores." I raise my eyebrows as I type the name in and wonder why he has switched his name from Juan to John. He laughs quietly. "It's easier, more American," he says. "And the password," I ask. "What should I type in?" He smiles, and says, "My password is 'success.'"

WORDS—I

During one of my observations of Mushutu's English class, the teacher gives an unexpected quiz to the class. Rather than see how Mushutu interacts in class, I sit in the back of a quiet room where students sweat over distinctions in *The Scarlet Letter.* I leave the class early because the students are quietly working on their exams. Shortly after the observation Mushutu and I have a familiar interchange, this time by e-mail, over the meaning of a word. Mushutu has an exceptional ability to learn a complex new word and then use it in a manner which is occasionally slightly off-meaning. He seems to delight in arguing with me over the meaning of words, and once he gets the proper interpretation he will use it correctly the next time we meet.

> Hello Professor Tierney,
> I apologize for what happened in English class. It was sort of anticlimactic. Indeed, a surprise! I never knew that it would be a test day. I am very sorry that it was a waste of your time. Oh, by the way, I scored high on the essay test. I hope I did not waste to much of your time on Wednesday. When am I seeing you again?
>
> Mushutu

> Hi Mushutu,
>
> I'm glad you got a good score on your essay. Do you think it was 'anticlimactic?' Let's discuss the meaning of that. . . .

> Hello Professor Tierney,
>
> I am sorry that I am consuming your time with these petty emails. Let me get to the point. I thought 'anticlimactic' meant that one anticipated something good and instead something inferior happened. I used 'anticlimactic' because I thought we would be discussing matters such as the 'politics of language.'
>
> I hope I did not butcher the meaning of 'anticlimactic' as I have done with many other words such as 'nihilist.' Till next time.
>
> Mushutu
>
> P.S. I am going to do my homework, now—not homeworks!!!

CRIME AND PUNISHMENT

Juan is waiting for me on a street corner to take me to his house. He is carrying a torn copy of *Crime and Punishment.* When I say that it is one of my favorite books, but very difficult, Juan smiles and says, "Yes. Difficult. But very good. Very sincere."

When we get to the gate of the apartment he pulls out a roll of keys and uses two of them to open the gate. We walk up the apartment's 11 steps and I notice that the wooden front door has a hole where the door knob should be. It swings back and forth, and he pushes it in to open it for me. I step into a dark foyer devoid of any furniture with one window that is partially detached from its moorings; two boys and a girl are hanging out the window as we walk by. Juan does not acknowledge the trio, and we seem invisible to them. When I leave the apartment, two of them are gone, and one of the boys is lying face down on the well-worn rug oblivious to the noise from the street or my departure as I step around him. A strong smell of urine emanates from the rug.

We walk down a dark hall, and Juan opens the door to his apartment with another key. He lives with his mother and Diego in one room with a small kitchen and bathroom. Two beds and a couch neatly frame three sides of the room. Juan's computer is crammed into a corner; the Virgin of Guadalupe is Juan's screensaver. A small TV is on as we enter, and his mother comes to shake my hand. Diego is a skinny 12-year-old who utters nothing except one-word answers to my questions as he tries simultaneously to watch *Scooby Doo* and his brother's interactions with this stranger.

The small TV is perched on a table surrounded by miniature figurines. A plastic Santa Claus with a guitar stands atop the TV and three separate Virgins of Guadalupe stand off to a side bookended by a small ballerina in a plastic skirt and a Mexican-looking Elvis with a mustache and dressed in white pants and a cape. Juan and I work on the computer looking at various classes he might take at a community college, and his mother eventually calls us into the kitchen for supper where she has retreated soon after I arrive.

The two windows in the apartment look out on an adjacent roof of a supermarket.

"It gets hot in the afternoon," Juan says as we go into the kitchen. "I like that it's quiet, not noisy. At night, when I'm sleepy it's easy. Sometimes there is noise outside, the halls, people, but it's quiet usually—except he snores," and he points to Diego.

Diego wrinkles his nose as he slides into his chair in the kitchen and reaches for a corn tortilla from a huge package his mother has taken from the refrigerator. She grabs Diego's hand and says to Juan in Spanish, "Give him some," pointing to me. We sit around a small Formica table that seats three. His mother motions for Juan to get the bucket from the bathroom which he turns upside down to use as his chair. We quietly work our way through the tortillas and a fish mixture with salsa bought from the supermarket next door. "He likes it," his mother says as I reach for my third helping. I speak in my fractured Spanish, and we talk about the difficulty of foreign languages.

Juan enjoys listening to my Spanish and says, "Your Spanish—it's like my English." I shake my head back and forth and say in Spanish, "No. Your English is much better. It's excellent." His mother laughs and takes Juan's free hand. He continues eating.

"This is special, yes," Juan eventually laughs. "Usually we just get our own meal. Sometimes I get it for him," motioning to Diego who is leaning back in his chair trying to monitor the antics of Scooby and his friends. We drink an orange-flavored juice and eventually turn to fresh grapes for dessert. His mother sits quietly, monitoring to make sure we each have enough and continually asks me if I like it. She says she has never learned English, that it's too hard. I ask Diego if he speaks Spanish and he nods his head up and down and says his Spanish is "ok"; Juan contradicts him and says "it's bad. His English is better if he studies his schoolwork." Diego ignores him and gets up and goes back into the room to watch the end of the movie, grabbing a handful of grapes on his way out. Juan's mother moves to clear the plastic dishes and Juan returns the bucket to the bathroom.

Mushutu's parents have moved from the Jungle to another area of Los Angeles that is still poor but less dangerous. "I don't feel threatened," he says as we park in front of the apartment complex, "it's not like, so scary here." The large complex is next to an AMC church and I ask if he ever attends. "O gosh, no. That's not our church. We go to an Ethiopian church that is about 15 minutes from here." He swings open the gate to a complex that has about 10 two-story buildings that are connected to one another by cement walkways. No one is outside, and I ask Mushutu if he knows anyone here or ever visits anybody his own age. "I would say that there are some kids my age here, but I don't see them, like, to be friends with. My little brother—my mother lets him play outside sometimes. But me, no."

"I know," I say. "You're too busy with your homeworks."

He grins. "Homework," he corrects me. "I'm a home-a-philiac."

I misunderstand him. "What?"

"Homeaphilia. I like staying home. Last weekend I came home from school Friday night and I didn't go outside until Monday morning. I was very busy."

At the back of the apartment complex, we climb to the second floor. He opens the door and says in English, "We're here." His sister is cooking in the kitchen, and his father stands and slips on a suit coat over a short-sleeved white shirt. After my experience with Juan's mom I have asked Mushutu on the way over if he is going to translate for me with his father because I don't speak Amharic.

"He wouldn't like that," he replies quickly. "That would be insulting—his son speaking for him. His fluency is not excellent, but linguistically he can speak English." Mushutu's mother is visiting her sister in Sacramento, and she has taken Mushutu's younger brother with her.

Mushutu's father is a quiet, dignified man with a thin mustache and a soft voice. His son is now as tall as he is, and he laughs about Mushutu: "My little boy is growing, growing, growing. I could not stay away from watching over my family." Nevertheless, he expresses regret at having left Ethiopia and concern for living in America. "I worked in a health clinic in my country," he tells me, "but here I work at night parking cars." He shakes his head back and forth and sits back on the living room couch. "My country, I think it's better for us, but my wife's problems. We came here. I had no other choice."

I ask him about his impression of Mushutu's school. Neither he nor his wife has visited the school, but they have driven by it and they have looked at his homework, even though he does it on his own. "He was in a very good school in Ethiopia. The best. This city. Are all schools like this? The sciences and the maths are very weak."

I mention that many of our schools are like the one Mushutu attends and comment how impressed I am with Mushutu.

His father says quietly, "He has always been like that. Even very young. He is very independent-minded, but no problems. A good boy. Very smart."

Mushutu's sister steps out from the kitchen and says, "Let's eat. The food is ready." Selam is 21 and very attractive, with shoulder-length brown hair, Mushutu's expressive brown eyes, and her father's quiet demeanor. She works two jobs as a cashier at different restaurants and expresses a desire to get a community college degree, but her passion is her religion. Mushutu explains to me many times that he worries about her because she is so religious. "She should get married, but she may be like a nun, like a saint," he says to me one day.

When Mushutu takes me to the bathroom to wash my hands he shows me the small room he shares with his younger brother; he points to the computer and laughingly whispers, "My screen saver is a soccer player, Renaldo, a Brazilian guy, but my sister said I should get rid of it because he's wearing shorts and instead put the Virgin Mary on it." "What did you do?" I ask. He moves over to the computer and flicks on the screen. Renaldo pops up.

A feast of Ethiopian food is waiting as we sit down at the table. Selam has made traditional bread—injera—rice, steamed vegetables, salad, large muffins, a bulgur-like stew, and eventually she offers fresh fruit for dessert. "No chicken, we have no chicken," his father says somewhat embarrassedly. "When my wife comes we will have a very good meal for you."

Mushutu and his sister sit quietly while his father and I talk. Toward the end of the meal I ask about Ethiopia and what it is like. His father smiles resignedly: "Everything is so rushed here. Mushutu is always in a hurry, always working. No time to relax." I look over to Mushutu, and he smiles sheepishly. Selam says, "In our country people are always visiting. There is time. You'll have coffee now." She gets up to make the coffee and Mushutu goes into the kitchen with her. His father says, "Yes, coffee, it's good. In our country we have three cups. It's a time to sit and talk with friends, with family."

Over the next half hour Selam serves a first, and then a second, and finally a third cup. We drink from mugs resembling espresso cups, and there is a light cardamom flavor to the dark mix. Mushutu sits quietly while his father and sister tell me about Addis Ababa. I ask them if they think they will return and his father says, "No jobs. Jobs are difficult. And we must wait for him to go to college."

Although he fully expects his son to go to college, he is mystified by the process. "In Ethiopia it's very clear. I know which university he would go to. But here there are so many institutions and some are so far." His daughter adds, "And the cost. Everything is so expensive here. He has to get a loan." "No," corrects Mushutu, "I need a grant. A fellowship. We have a low-income level. When I fill out the FAFSA, I must be sure to get grant or monies. We can't pay."

Eventually I take my leave. As I walk to the door Mushutu's father takes my hand. "Please help my son," he says, "He is a good boy. He must go to college."

OUR DEAR BROTHER'S DEATH THY MEMORY BE GREEN

I have been observing Juan's government class and am headed to world literature; unfortunately, I have gotten lost and am in the middle of the quad as students run toward their next class. One student brushes by me, and I drop the papers with my notes. As I bend to pick them up, the bell rings, signaling that everyone should be in class. Memories of hall passes and being sent to the principal's office start to flood in on me, and I hear a voice call out, "Mr. Mr! Come this way, quick." Juan is standing at the entrance of the building I have just exited and motions to me with his right hand. I run over and we race up to the second floor. "We are late," he says and we enter the classroom just as Mrs. Brahim starts to close the door. "This is the teacher I mentioned," Juan says pointing at me. She nods and signals an empty seat for me to sit in at the back of the class. Juan slides into a seat up front close to Mrs. Brahim's desk. Students continue chatting amongst themselves while Juan quietly gets out his notebook and book, speaking to no one.

As I catch my breath Mrs. Brahim begins class with a quick review of where they are in *Hamlet*. "Ok, now I hope you all remember the difference between a comedy and tragedy. We discussed this last time. Now who knows the difference and don't tell me that one is happy and one is sad," she says looking over at a boy who, I eventually discover, seems to have smart-aleck answers for Mrs. Brahim's questions, but whom she also likes. A thin girl hesitantly raises her hand and mumbles a response about tragedy having to do with a disaster that symbolizes something more than a character's death.

The class is supposed to have read the text, and they watched the movie starring Mel Gibson last week. In the ensuing period Mrs. Brahim speaks 80% of the time and less than half of the students in the class make up the remaining 20% of conversation. The students remain attentive, although one fellow is reading *A Clockwork Orange,* another is doing his homework for the next class, and two girls are passing notes about a boy who sits near them. Juan maintains his attention on Mrs. Brahim. "Now take out your study questions, and let's get to work," she says.

Juan takes out his notebook and dutifully turns to filling in the answers. He raises his hand to ask a question. She comes over to him, and he asks quietly, "What's a Dane?" "Excuse me," she says, "I can't hear you, Juan." "A Dane," he says, pointing to the study questions. "What's a Dane?" She tries to encourage him, "A Mexican is from Mexico. A Dane is from . . . ?" "O. Yes. Danish. Someone from Danish." "Yes. Right. Denmark. Hamlet was from Denmark," and she turns back to the class and begins to write the family history of Hamlet on the blackboard. "You don't take notes," she says to the class. "That's why you forget things. You have to get this down." From the back of the room I can't see to whom Polonius is supposed to be related.

Juan does not say anything else in class and dutifully records everything the teacher writes on the board. I speak with Juan after the class, and we discuss *Hamlet* and his understanding of the text. "O, yes, I like *Hamlet* very much" he says. "The movie was good. Mel Gibson. The words are difficult, sometimes. [Mrs. Brahim] gave us a paper summary with different words so it does not become difficult for us."

I flip through the book he has given me and notice various Spanish words penciled in the margins. "Did you write these words in the book," I ask, wondering about his linguistic code switching.

"Yeah, but I erase them when I am done," he responds, worried that I am angry he has defaced a school book.

"Do you normally write in Spanish?"

"Well, if I don't understand the word I write it on a separate paper. I write the word in Spanish if I understand it when she says it. It's easier to understand that way."

I turn to the page where they have left off at the end of class and say, "So let's go over some phrases. Listen to this: 'Though yet, of Hamlet, our dear brother's death the memory be green.' What do you think that means, Juan, 'the memory be green?'"

"Well you see that's the problem in a way. Some types of English—it's not only reading it's like the words sometimes aren't even English. I have to find the definition of each word and then think about the meaning, and it takes time."

"The memory be green. What do you think 'green' represents?"

"Well, depending what green represents."

"What does green represent?"

"Poison," Juan ventures? "It means poison?"

In later weeks I discover that Juan spends a great deal of his free time reading texts his teachers have given him, and he then tries to understand first the difficult words, and then their meaning. He never speaks to anyone about the texts, even though he enjoys trying to puzzle out meanings. He rarely speaks in class because he is "calm" and he is afraid of saying something "dumb."

"When do you see green, Juan?" I ask.

"Christmas day," he says animatedly. "It means we should remember like days at Christmas?" he ventures.

"When else do you see green in a season? Do you see green in the winter?"

"No."

"When do you see it?"

"Summer."

"Ok, good. We also see it in spring, right?"

"Correct, in the spring."

I continue to read: "'The memory be green and that it us be fitted to bear our hearts in grief, and our whole kingdom to be contracted in one brow of woe.' Does this make sense?"

"Not too much," he admits.

I read on: "'Have we, as twere with a defeated joy with an auspicious and a dropping eye with mirth in funeral and with dirge in marriage, in equal scale weighing delight and dole.' Phwew! It's tough, huh? It's a very good story, though."

"I think the movie, it's better."

AIDS

It's the Sunday of AIDS Walk L.A. Mushutu is wearing the t-shirt he got at the start of the event as he walks with 40 other students and his teacher. He has gotten the t-shirt for raising $400 for AIDS prevention. During the walk Mushutu talks with his teacher and another adult; the rest of the students walk together in small groups. It's a festive atmosphere; there is a marching band, lots of applause from onlookers. Hollywood stars occasionally punctuate the route to encourage the walkers. This is Mushutu's first AIDS walk, although he learned about AIDS in Ethiopia.

"My teacher said 'would you like to do the walk?' He said we would get community service and all of that. I did something like it in Ethiopia because so many people are infected with HIV. The whole idea was to help out, and even if I didn't get any community service credit, I'd still do it. It's important."

Mushutu has raised more than any of the other students by getting people to sponsor him in the walk. He has gone to a mall on Saturdays and to USC and just walked up to people and asked them to give him some money. He has had only one problem.

"Most people kind of know about it, about AIDS Walk, so they sponsor me because I'm a kid and they want to help. I try to be funny when I ask people so they don't grow scared. I would say it's easy to talk to people, to just ask them, and get them to sign up, to pledge money and get their phone numbers. Some of them backed away, like 'who are you,' but most people just signed right up. My legs were kind of hurting when I got home because I ran around so much, but it was fun, yeah. I did it by myself."

"I was only disappointed by one guy, like he was, he was like, I asked him if he would like to sponsor me and he said, 'that's kind of impromptu isn't it?' Then he waited when I didn't say anything and he said, "Do you know what impromptu means?" Of course I know what impromptu means! I said yes and then he said, 'It means spontaneous.' Okay, so I was like why do you have to tell me that if I already said I knew what it meant. I don't like it that he acted like I was a stupid kid or something. But he was the only guy who wasn't nice."

"I checked out information about AIDS on the Web and it's like too many people are dying. The predominant demographics are horrible about how many people die. It's very harsh. I would say that we all have to do something. It is very catastrophic."

FRIDA AND DIEGO

Juan tells me he typically rents one movie for Diego and one for himself on Friday nights. "We watch videos. It's good for him. He likes them. I sometimes will watch them, but his movie I put in and then do the computer. He gets tired and goes to sleep and I watch mine." Sometimes he talks about movies that affected him.

"When I was working on Sunday I thought about this movie I saw last week. My brother got the Matrix movie, but I rented another video; it's about the life of Diego Rivera and his wife, Frida Kahlo. It was of interest. Diego Rivera was not an honest man. He cheated on his wife, on Frida. That was not responsible."

I ask Juan about his own ideas about relationships. I wonder if he will get married or have children. He hesitates as he forms his ideas, but he has thought about these questions a great deal, and we return to this topic numerous times.

"I like to think when I work. It's quiet and it makes the time go fastly. I thought about relationships and me. If I had a son I would call him 'Gustavo.' It's a beautiful name. He doesn't need to be named after me. I am not ready to be a father. I need to know myself. I don't love myself, and I'd have to do that. Maybe I won't have a baby ever. It's difficult. Sometimes I don't like what I do. You have to be responsible, take care of the child, be able to give love, and I don't think I can do that right now."

"When you give love and it breaks, when you just leave, or stop loving, in a sense, it hurts the child, and that's not good. It's a big problem."

"I work hard, and I am modest and I don't get angry. I think those are good. In a way, my problem is I don't know how to talk to people, especially girls. If I am to marry I need to be able to give advice so she can feel comfortable and know what to do, and I need to listen to her. If we have a child we need to be strong and I need to make her feel ok; I don't mean physical love. Physical love isn't love; it's desire. It's wrong because you don't think about the consequences. By love I mean 'agape.' In a sense, it means spiritual love, true love. I don't know how to do that."

COLLEGE APPLICATIONS

Although both boys desperately want to go to college, Mushutu and Juan have wildly different understandings and approaches to navigating the college application process. Mushutu has taken the SAT numerous times and continues to try to improve his score so that he reaches his goal of 1400. "The upward bound counselor mentioned that at the really good schools, MIT and ones like that, I need over 1400 so that's my goal." Juan has never spoken to anyone about the SAT and once he got 660, he never took it again.

Mushutu is aware of which classes will propel him into a good college, and he undertakes activities that will make his college application appear stronger. Although he mentions, for example, that he participated in the AIDS Walk because it was important, he also had figured out that he could list it as an activity on his college application. Juan tends to take classes that are assigned to him by a counselor with whom he rarely meets. As a consequence, he ends up in a course such as the advanced placement class for which he is not qualified and in which he has no interest. Because he works 24 hours a week, he also has little time for extracurricular activities, and no one has reached out to him offering him advice. He is late for school in part because he gets home from work twice a week after midnight, and he is tired in the morning. His mother will have left for work by the time he should get up, so he has no one to help him. Indeed, he believes he is responsible for helping Diego to go to school, which further slows him down. The result is chronic late attendance. His response has been to take makeup classes outside of the regular school year to see if he might improve his grades by effectively repeating classes where he has gotten a D or an F.

Mushutu is able to envision college in a way that is difficult for Juan. When I ask them what is their ideal college Mushutu states:

> Pretty much I want a small professor to student ratio, kind of a small school, I would say; I don't want it to be big. It can be big as long as the classes are not that big, yeah. And I want to know everybody and who to ask. It's important to be able to ask people for advice so I need to not feel lost, like o my gosh I wonder if they will like me. I'm good in math and science and I think I might like engineering. I am hoping to go to MIT for my doctorate and master's, I saw a show about it and looked it up on the Internet, so I'd like something different for my undergraduate. I have to feel comfortable, not like I'm lost or just this kid who wanders around. I'm tenacious, so I will work hard, but the college has to help, too. I haven't visited colleges, I haven't the money, so I'm not sure actually what I want, but that's what I think. I'm superstitious, but I think I'll be able to get where I want.

Juan has a less focused approach to what he wants:

> I think I want to be a paralegal. I think that's what I want. I know a bachelor's is better so I want to go to a university. I'm not sure what I need to take, but I think someone will help me when I get there, perhaps.

Although Juan speaks about the desire to apply for college, and he has received printed instructions about what he needs to do, he still ends up in my office the day before the application for California State University is due without having started it. "It's very confusing," he says. No one in his high school has sat down with him and gone over how to apply for college throughout his high school career. When I ask him what he thinks he will major in, he is unsure what I mean. Like Mushutu, none of Juan's relatives or extended family has ever applied for college. Juan is the only person in his family to have graduated from grammar school. Neither Mushutu nor Juan speak about their parents or siblings when they talk about how to apply for college; the processes and decisions are left to each youth. After Juan has applied, he waits expectantly to hear about his application and is upset when he is rejected, even though we have discussed the problems with his academic record and SAT scores. "I know, they are not good," he tells me, "but I want to go to college. That is my dream." He then turns to community college Web sites and begins to think about the difficult process of taking classes during the day and "getting a job" during the evening. Because he remains undocumented he also recognizes the clock is ticking: Diego will turn 18 in a few years and Juan will be unable to use Diego's social security number to gain employment.

Mushutu will be a senior next year. Because he has excellent grades and a superb SAT score—despite his perception—he has started to receive letters of interest from colleges. He is "sanguine" he tells me, about the letters:

> I know what they are doing. You can get flattered when you get letters from schools telling you they want you to apply, but I know what they are doing. I'm like at first, "o my gosh, I've got a letter from a college that I've never heard of. I must be good, yeah." But then I know that because I'm a black kid they just want me to apply for their numbers. I have to figure out what's for me, I would say, not for them.

LA MIGRA—I

> In the wake of U.S. Border Patrol arrests in the Inland Empire, heavily Latino neighborhoods and shopping districts were muted Friday as many fearful residents changed their routines to avoid rumored illegal-immigrant sweeps. "They're nervous. Everyone is afraid," said Rene Morales. "There's fear all over Los Angeles."
>
> *Los Angeles Times*, June 12, 2004, B1

THE BEEPER

Juan's boss gives him a beeper when he goes to work so that Juan can move around the hotel and do odd jobs when he is beeped. During Intersession his boss has told Juan to take the beeper home with him; if there is additional work his boss will beep Juan. On Saturday Juan goes to work, but forgets his beeper and calls his mom and asks her to bring the beeper to him. He tells her to take the blue line to 7th and Figueroa where he will be waiting for her.

The subway doors open and she hands Juan the beeper and he heads outside. An officer stops him in the tunnel and asks to see his ticket.

"I don't have a ticket. I was waiting for my mom to give me something."

The officer asks Juan what he was doing and he tells him that he is taking a class; the officer writes a ticket and tells him to go to a judge and pay a fine for not having bought a subway token.

"I can't tell him that I was working, or I could get in trouble," Juan explains. "It's always a big problem."

When he finally goes to court he has to skip school and the judge is impressed that he is carrying books. "I'm surprised," she says, "that you've got schoolbooks with you. I don't see many juveniles like you carrying books. But you shouldn't have boarded a train without a ticket. And this is your second offense. The fine is ninety dollars. Don't do it again, Mr. Flores."

He pays the fine in cash and returns to school.

LA MIGRA—II

An email from Juan on June 18:

> I have question. If I or an individual is arrested by the INS, but that person have lived more than a decade can he/she legalize its status because of the years the individual has lived here?
>
> Should a person give their name when asked? Or give information where they lived?
>
> Take Care

THE CONUNDRUM OF ADVANCED PLACEMENT

Mushutu is taking AP English, U.S. history, and chemistry. In large part because of the preparation he has done on his own for the SAT his writing skills have improved dramatically, and he expects to do well on the English exam. He also has a facility for learning and keeping facts that has put him in good stead for English and history. His vocabulary has improved and he has a solid understanding of the myriad facts that make up U.S. history. I quiz him one day for an hour. Although he has been in the United States for less than five years he answers every question correctly about eighteenth- century American history. "I've had a few 3's and 4's," his history teacher tells me, "Mushutu may be my first 5 this year. He's that good."

Mushutu's stumbling block is chemistry. In contrast to English and history, he is unable to study such abstract concepts on his own and instead needs terms explained to him. Throughout the year he grows impatient with teachers and classmates who are not motivated, especially in math and science.

"I don't understand some kids," he says. "I think when you commit yourself to something you should do it. It's a promise and you should keep your commitments. I don't want to speculate why students don't work hard, but I think teachers should be harder, they should expect more of us and be less circumspect in their criticism."

He continually returns to his concerns about chemistry. "I don't feel we are moving at the right progress," he informs me mid-semester. "It's too slow. Like in U.S. history our teacher gives us bunches of assignments and papers to do, reading. He tries to go over things with us and he meets with us on Saturdays and he will spend one whole week before the exam reviewing with us. But in chemistry some kids don't know very much and they don't work hard, so we go slow. And the teacher, he's not very demanding. He kind of tries to make it easy, not good easy, but like lazy easy, full of sloth, yeah."

Before the AP exam he summarizes his feelings: "It's a conundrum. Do you bring everyone along, which takes time and slows us down, or do you teach at the rate that prepares you for the AP exam. We are bringing everyone along. It's too slow. That's the problem of a magnet. It puts everyone in."

After the AP exams have concluded Mushutu emails me:

Hello Prof. Tierney,

How is everything going? My AP tests have sort of went well. I think I did better than expected in English and History. They were sort of easy. Chemistry was not good. I am just wondering, how much importance do our AP scores have in the college admission process?

We did not even cover a quarter of what we are supposed to know for Chemistry! So, if I get a horrible score on it, does it mean it might jeopardize my acceptance to good colleges? Besides, I am intending to study science and it might sound very ironic that I might do worse in science than humanities.

Well, that is it about Chemistry. The fact that I might not do well on it sort of saddens and angers me at the same time.

Turning to another subject, I just wanted to remind you of our discussion. When are we supposed to use "superstitious"? I thought I would revive the topic. I guess that will be the end of my email. I hope to hear from you.

Mushutu

Mushutu finds out his scores and comes by my office to tell me. "Actually," he smiles, "they're not bad."

Chemistry—3
U.S. History—5
English—5

MARBURY V MADISON

Juan sits near the front of his AP class and quietly writes notes as the teacher talks. The class lesson is about the Supreme Court, and the students appear mildly interested. The teacher good-humoredly says, "Ok, now let's open our books to the section on *Marbury v Madison*. Who knows why this Supreme Court case is important? Who's going to give me a good answer?" The teacher has created the classroom as a horseshoe and turns around repeatedly, rubbing his hands back and forth. "Anthony, how about you? What do you remember?" Anthony apparently doesn't remember too much because he shrugs his shoulders. His friend sitting next to him says, "Yo. Mr. Forrester. Me. Ask me." "Why don't we have Anthony read the section in our books on it first. Anthony could you read it for us. A loud voice, Anthony, so we can all hear that voice of yours."

The students open their books to the assigned page and one girl good-naturedly blurts out, "It's about who's in charge. Like is the president all-mighty or what." As she speaks and Anthony begins to read, Juan has flipped to the back of the book and searches through the index. After a few minutes he opens his textbook, but he is clearly on a different page from everyone else; they are at the front of the book and he is toward the middle. After class I ask him what was going on.

"The book. They are out of books. I entered late and they gave me an old book. So I have to look it up in the index when Mr. Forrester starts a topic. It's not too bad," he shrugs. "The topics, I can usually find them in the index. It just takes me a minute. Madison, he was a president?"

BLACK HAWK DOWN

Mushutu sees *Black Hawk Down* with his history class and he decides to review the history of Somalia through the Internet. "I mean," he says, "I felt bad for the American soldiers, but it shows them just getting blown away. It's just so Hollywood, so Hollywood. You can represent both sides and not be so one-sided. I went to the Internet to try to understand the Somali side of it. Americans seem to think they're the only ones, like the others don't count, like it's only Americans who are important. When I look at the Internet and see all the pain in Somalia I think 'gosh, what if that happens to me?' It was very horrific."

Juan has a similar assessment of America and he has reached his judgment by thinking about what it means to be an immigrant in the United States. He arrives to one interview after a class where the discussion has been about immigration.

"Immigration is a big huge problem," says Juan. "Especially for America since there's so many immigrants coming in to the United States with coyotes."

"What do you think we should do?"

"Well for me I think we should legalize people that have been here their entire life, like for me. We are not terrorists as people think. We came for one reason: to do better and to have a better life. We help the economy."

"What would you say to a guy that said you came here illegally?

"Illegally. In a sense, basically it's the truth. I came here illegally, but I came for a reason, not to take away from your country but to have a better life and education and to make your country better. America likes some people more than others. They don't like Mexicans."

Although Mushutu and Juan have not spoken with one another, they define their position in the world in quite similar ways. Mushutu says one day, "When I was a little kid I used to think that America was like a dream land. But now that I'm here I don't like that Americans are so proud, that they act so superior. They are an empire, and they are only 300 years old; they don't even recognize that a country like Ethiopia is almost the oldest in the world. In Ethiopia people are hopeful for one another; here, it's more like you're on your own, more individual. I like learning American history, though. The one thing I enjoy is that you can debate American history. I usually argue with my history teacher and I like that things are open to argument, to argumentation. But it's like Americans are afraid or something, I would say. Maybe we'll overcome this fear. It's a big problem."

Juan is less optimistic: "People need to help the poor. That's my beliefs. If you are hungry then I should feed you. The United States doesn't think like that. They think we are criminals."

FINANCIAL AID

Because Juan and Mushutu are poor they constantly worry about how they are going to pay for college. Indeed, many of the pre-college activities that are necessary are impossible for them to afford. Mushutu tries to take an SAT exam in the spring, but because the counselor has been out sick he cannot get a fee waiver. We complete Juan's application to CSU at the last minute, and he has no time to get a fee waiver. Because he is undocumented and has neither a credit card nor a checking account, he has no way to pay the fee, so I pay it for him. Mushutu never considers taking an SAT prep class such as Stanley Kaplan because "it's just too much money." Juan would like to visit college campuses but can't take time off from his job for one weekend to make the trip. Mushutu would like to take a summer course for college credit on a college campus but the cost—$4,000—is absurdly out of reach. Juan tells me one day that someone called him about college scholarships:

> They were having a meeting on Saturday like an orientation. It's a big company, a scholarship company. My mother and I, we paid fifty dollars, and went to the Holiday Inn. I translated for her. They gave me two options. They gave me a list of scholarships, like five hundred, and they said I could apply if I sent five hundred letters. The second option was to pay them one hundred forty nine dollars and the people would do the work for me and narrow the list down to match me up with the application. It's too expensive so we haven't done nothing.

Mushutu is leery of people and Web sites "who waste your time and want you to pay them money. I don't think you get very much in return." He thinks a great deal about who should pay for college and he agrees with Juan's conception of America:

> Take me, for example. I am not able to afford four thousand dollars a year. I don't even think I can afford one thousand. If you want your country to develop as a team you have to pull all those people along and it's like getting the whole community to work together. We need to help out the less fortunate and help each other.

Neither of them can envision taking out a loan. "I don't want debt," says Mushutu. "I can't afford it and won't do it." Juan adds, "Debts are bad. I couldn't get it anyway—no residency status."

The law in California has tried to help people like Juan, but a half measure turns out to be no measure at all. The law enables him to pay in-state tuition if he attends a CSU or UC, but he is ineligible for financial aid. Instead of the $4,000 that an out-of-state student has to pay, he is able to pay $1,500. "I know that the money is less, yes, but it's still too much for me," says Juan. "I have to help my mom."

LA MIGRA—III

Juan's paycheck every two weeks: $561.89

The following is deducted:

Federal withholding:	$55.44
FICA:	$34.84
Medicare:	$8.15
CA withholding:	$6.58
CA disability:	$6.65
Total taxes deducted:	$111.64

Juan's take home pay is $450.25 every two weeks.

Twenty percent of every paycheck are taxes that he will never claim or use, such as Medicare or tuition for public higher education.

"You see, I give the United States money," Juan laughs. "They just don't know it."

WORDS–II

Mushutu comes to speak with me on a quiet Friday afternoon. The following day I need to give a talk to a group concerned with financial aid and access. I ask him what I should say, what I should tell them.

He pauses and looks out the window. He turns to face me and his left hand starts to cut through the air to make a point, his index finger leading the way. "Tell them," he says, "Tell them, I am indignant."

I sigh. Here we go again. Another vocabulary lesson. "Indignant, Mushutu? Why indignant."

He looks out the window again and is quiet. He turns back and says animatedly, "Yes, indignant. Indignant. This is America. We have no books. The teachers aren't serious, some of them. People say that college is important but it's not possible; it costs too much. We aren't prepared right. This is America. Yes. Yes. I am indignant."

He returns to looking out the window and silence fills the room. He looks back at me and smiles and asks, "Correct?"

"Yes, Mushutu, you are correct. You should be indignant."

He looks, momentarily, content.

4

· · · · · · · · · · · ·

Julia E. Colyar

Big Ideas, Small Details

JENNY ACEVEDO

· · ·

On an assignment for her psychology class, Jenny describes herself: "I have a personality of a Movie Star and I am a ray of sunshine that secretly wonders why I am not famous yet. I do not get annoyed with people very easily and I can handle stressful situations with grace . . . I am friendly, charming, and great with people . . . I like making my environment cozy and hospitable . . . I never shy away from asserting my ideas and opinions, and I encourage others to do the same."

QUINCEAÑERA—PART I

The first images are blurred, chaotic. Yellow, white lace, arms, and what looks like kitchen cabinets. Voices in the background talk over one another in Spanish, and the camera moves in and out, looking for focus. Finally, the videographer steadies the camera and settles on Jenny. She is standing in the family room of her house, and three women are kneeling at her feet, smoothing the hem of Jenny's long dress, tugging at the edges and evening out the pattern of beads. Jenny stands motionless, arms slightly raised from her sides, looking vaguely uncomfortable. Her Quinceañera gown is heavy, made from thick yellow satin and extensively adorned with beads shaped into large sunflowers. The mass and celebration have not even started yet—she is dressing with the help of her mother and aunts—and she is already fatigued, on the verge of tears. She looks directly into the camera, and her expression shifts:

"Don't turn that on yet. I don't even have my hair done." She reaches out, swatting at the video camera, smiling and laughing.

The videotape of Jenny's Quinceañera celebration chronicles a day of changing emotions. As we sit on the couch in Jenny's house, she warns me that the videotape is full of crying. "I cried like seven times in this tape; three times before we even left the house!" For Jenny and her family, the ceremony is sacred and significant, a traditional Mexican celebration marking a young woman's 15th birthday. This ceremony not only announces Jenny's 15th year, it is also a symbolic moment for her family, for the difficulties of their immigration to the United States and the successes they have worked hard to achieve. It marks Jenny's connection to her culture and its rituals; it celebrates Jenny's passage into adulthood and recognizes the importance of her family in the journey. As we sit and watch the video, Jenny narrates the happenings; the players are speaking Spanish, and I know only a few words. She tells me about her dress—custom made just for her by a dressmaker in Los Angeles—the colors she has chosen—yellow, not the traditional white, detailed with thousands of colorful beads—and her shoes. She runs to her closet to show me the shoes firsthand. "Well," she explains, "these are the second shoes. I wore shoes with a low heel to start, then I change into these shoes. You'll see it later—my stepdad gives me the second shoes to wear, you know, because they are like adult shoes. With a higher heel." Jenny sets her shoes on the coffee table in the living room, and we turn back to the video. "Look," she says, "here's my mom crying. She cries all day too."

MARIANNA AND THE PEPSI GUY

Marianna was mean to all the boys, sort of shy. She was the third oldest of seven children (four girls and three boys); she lived with her family in San Nicholas de los Augustinos, a small town in central Mexico. When she was 14, she used to spend the afternoon sitting with her sisters and friends outside the local grocery. They waited for the young man who filled the vending machines with soft drinks; "Here comes the Pepsi guy," they would say.

The Pepsi guy, Guillermo, was 17 years old and lived with his grandparents in a neighboring town called Salvatierra. At first he didn't know what to make of Marianna; she was standoffish, seemed uninterested. She just sat on the wooden steps, never looking at him as he filled the machines with Pepsi and orange soda. The other girls twittered and laughed, but Marianna was demure. How they ever got together, no one is really sure. But by the time Marianna was 15, the two were married. Soon after, a daughter, Yeni, was born—a month premature, sickly with jaundice and anemia. Both Yeni and Marianna almost died.

When Yeni was nine months old, Marianna and Guillermo immigrated to the United States, Guillermo crossing first and his wife and daughter soon following. Marianna paid the coyote $500 to guide her and Yeni, crossing the border through Tijuana on foot. On their first attempt, the two were caught and arrested by immigration officers. They were sent back across the border where they gathered their resources for another attempt. After a week of heavy rain and waiting, Marianna, Yeni, and their guide tried again. This time, they made it. Guillermo, Marianna and Yeni settled in the San Jose area of California with several family members, all in the same large house. "Yeni" became "Jenny," the Americanized version of her Mexican name.

Each family in the house had a bedroom. Marianna remembers those first years in the United States:

> We left Mexico because we wanted more job opportunities; it was hard in Mexico, you know, not working. We had plans to come here and work, to open a business. So we came and we rented a house all together. So many people! It was fun, so . . . We all had one room, bedroom, and then we shared the kitchen. So we ate all together, one big family. Guillermo found a job doing construction, and he was working a lot. Too much. It was hard.

The extended family lived for four years in the big house before the separate families could afford to move into their own homes. "Sometimes we drive by the big house," Marianna tells me, "it looks the same."

When Jenny was five years old, she and her parents moved out of the big house and into a small apartment in the same neighborhood. Guillermo continued to work too much, and Jenny started pre-school at Wilson Elementary. This is where she learned to speak English: "We had a bilingual class, I guess. It is hard to remember." By the time she was in kindergarten, she was already reading in English. She didn't learn to read and write in Spanish until high school, when she had to enroll in foreign language classes. "Yeah," she says, "I guess I had it pretty easy, really. I learned English really fast, like I switched into English fast. I used to watch *Barney, Sesame Street,* and Freddy Krueger . . . I was kind of a weird little kid." When her parents would ask her what she wanted to be when she grew up, Jenny answered: "teacher, 'cause all my teachers were nice."

Not long after Jenny started attending Wilson Elementary School, her parents separated and later divorced. Jenny and her mother moved into another apartment with a friend; they shared the one-bedroom apartment with three others. Marianna worked at Target and tried to make ends meet, but she barely earned enough money to help pay the rent. "That was hard," Jenny tells me:

My mom, she's like really amazing. That's where I get my strength. Sometimes all we had to eat for a whole day was a hardboiled egg that we had to split. But I don't remember being hungry, you know, my needs were fulfilled . . . I just remember all the times I looked at my mom and thought "wow, I love her so much." Sometimes we look at each other when we're sitting around the table at home, all this food—rice and meat and everything—and I know we're thinking the same thing: "Remember when we just had the egg?"

Jenny says she uses these past hardships to look forward to the future. "Bad things brought good things," she tells me.

QUINCEAÑERA—PART II

The living room where we watch the Quinceañera video is long and rectangular in shape; the television fills one of the smaller walls—the screen must be about 72 inches—and a long couch lines one of the adjacent walls. Jenny sits in one of the end sections which opens up into a recliner. On the coffee table, there are bowls of popcorn and Cheetos, leftovers, Jenny tells me, from one of the afternoon "parties" her brothers and sister had with their grandfather. On the screen, Jenny is dancing with her stepfather, Carlos. "It was like a dream," she tells me. "I mean, the whole day. Some girls have their 15 just for the party, but I wanted to have a mass. It's like you're stepping into whatever you're gonna be." Jenny glances back to the TV and continues:

"You can't tell here, but Carlos is crying too. Everyone cried! It was really a big deal because I told Carlos, a couple weeks before, that I wanted to have my dance with him, not my real dad. Actually, I didn't even invite my dad to the party—just to the mass. I told Carlos, 'you're the one who has watched me grow up, you're going to be the one to support me in what I'll become.' And I think he was happy. But really, Carlos and my mom are the ones who were really there for me."

Marianna met Carlos through one of her sisters, and the two married when Jenny was in 6th grade. Carlos came to the United States from Guadalajara when he was 15; with his family, he settled in Monterey and went to school. Carlos had recently started his own cleaning business, and it was thriving. In addition to the local customers, Carlos also developed business relationships in Sacramento. The family grew as well: Serena was born in 1998, followed by twin boys—Carlos Jr. and Tony—in 2001. Suddenly, Jenny had brothers and sisters. "I was an only child till I was like 11," she explains. "But I think I became more open when Serena was born. She definitely made me a lot happier."

Tony and Carlos Jr. were not yet a year old when Jenny had her Quinceañera; their struggle to stand still for the photographer is documented in the video. Marianna holds one of the boys and tries to look at the camera while the other slumps down onto the floor—I can't tell the boys apart, so I ask Jenny which of them is causing trouble. "Oh, that's Carlos Jr. Tony is always really quiet, like he's shy. My aunts say he's just like my mom." Finally, they convince the little boy to stand up and smile for the camera. Jenny stands in the middle.

As a 9th grader, Jenny started school at San Pasqual High, and the family moved to a larger house in Laurel City. Carlos and Marianna ran the family business from their home office, and Marianna began taking classes in the mornings at a local community college. When her classes got harder in her sophomore year, Jenny thought: "You know, if all these people want to go [to college], what are my chances? I don't want to go to a community college, though—I don't need to."

Jenny pushes herself in school, enrolling in the most challenging curriculum she can. "I don't watch TV," she tells me. "Never did. When I'm not busy doing anything, I'm like 'what am I doing?' and I just have to get busy. I like to be busy, you know?" She plays soccer and volleyball, and participates in MESA (Mathematics, Engineering, Science Achievement), a state-supported college preparation program for underrepresented students seeking careers in math and science. Though Jenny's interests are more varied than math and science, she still enjoys the club's activities and the advisement she receives from her MESA counselors. "I take myself really seriously," she explains. "I'm always pushing. And everyone knows, you know? The whole family knows that I'm gonna go to college, and that's a lot of pressure. Some people say 'you can't do it,' and that just makes me want to do it more." She is the oldest daughter and granddaughter, and she will be the first in her family to go to college.

The video ends with a shot that pans away from Jenny dancing—she is enveloped in a circle, surrounded by a group of her friends and cousins. "I was *soooo* tired then," she tells me. "Look at my arms; I can barely move." As she rewinds the tape, we make plans to get some dinner; she has a favorite restaurant in town that makes great tacos. Just then, the front door opens and Tony and Carlos Jr. tumble in, ice-cream dried on their faces. Their grandfather—Marianna's father—follows, yelling at them in Spanish. When he sees me sitting on the couch, he stops and looks at Jenny. "This is my grandfather," she introduces. "Papa, this is the lady I was telling you about."

SAN PASQUAL HIGH SCHOOL

September 26, 2003. A bell sounds to announce the beginning of the day's last class. A voice comes over the loud speaker: "Attention please. All students are to clear the hallways for 7th period. And just a reminder: we have our first football games, JV and Varsity, on our new field tonight. Go Tigers!" Girls in cheerleading uniforms and boys wearing jerseys for the local professional baseball team file into class, talking loudly as they make their way to a desk. Despite the overhead announcement, the hallways are active; students hover in small groups in between the school buildings. The classroom I'm sitting in is covered with posters: Che Guevara, Frida Kahlo, Cesar Chavez, and pictures of students in formal dress posed in front of blue backgrounds at the winter dance and last year's prom. There's a flag for the United Farm Workers on one wall, and postcards from various colleges: UCLA, Cal Berkeley, Nebraska, and Stanford.

Jenny hurries into the classroom just as the tardy bell rings. Her tan boots click on the concrete as she walks—the boots have a heel of about two inches, which makes her stand at nearly 5 feet tall. She turns in my direction, her long dark ponytail following the movement of her head, and catches my eye. Her smile is bright, and her brown eyes light up with greeting. "We're meeting today, right?" she asks.

School started two weeks ago, and everyone is already worrying about college applications. After school, I follow Jenny to the library where she checks her email. One of the AVID classes is using the library computers as well, completing a "college check list" activity designed by Ms. Hong. All the students are stooped over computers, looking at Web pages for Harvard, San Jose State, and the College Board. While Jenny checks her Yahoo email account, I overhear an exchange between a senior and Ms. Hong:

Student: I need to register for the SAT II.

Ms. Hong: But today is the deadline!

Student: Are you serious?

Ms. Hong: Yes! Why do you think I've been freaking out here?! Look, sit here and do the registration on-line. You have a couple of hours to finish it.

The student looks in my direction, and we make eye contact; she smiles and raises her eye brows in a look of anxiety. Ms. Hong has already pulled up the registration Web site on a computer for her.

When Jenny opens her email, she has a message from David Matos, an admissions counselor from UC Berkeley. Though college admissions staff don't usually advise students about their applications, Matos has been a great resource for Jenny. "I've read your essay," he says, "and you need to put more of yourself into it. Don't think that everyone does what you do." Jenny has been working on her essay for a month already; she's revised it three times. The last time David read it, he crossed out the entire first page and said "you've told me nothing." Jenny closes the message and sighs heavily. "Again," she says, halfway between a question and a statement. "Does it bother you, his reaction?" I ask. "No, it's just something you gotta take. That's his job, he rips apart the essay." She shuts down the computer and takes a Sprite out of her backpack.

At the beginning of the school year, UC Berkeley is her first choice as a place to attend college. She has applied for an "Incentive Award," which is given to one student from her high school who will attend Berkeley. The scholarship provides $28,000 per year for four years; Jenny has made it through the first round of applications—at the school level—and her name has been forwarded with five others to Berkeley. "Ms. Jimenez called and let me know about the nomination," she tells me. "I was like, 'wow.' It's cool, you know?" And she's also planning to send applications to Stanford, Harvard, Santa Clara, Brown, UC Santa Barbara, UC Davis, UC San Diego, and probably others as well. She will get waivers for all the application fees, and she will apply as if her success as a student depends on the number of acceptance letters.

A ROOM WITH A VIEW

The library is on the second floor, and along one wall are large picture windows that overlook the student parking lot, the construction site for the new fine arts building, and the mountains in the distance. Jenny slings her backpack across her shoulders and points: "You see that?" she says, motioning toward a stop light just beyond the school's gates where cars are streaming into the afternoon. "White kids, rich kids, leave the school and turn left," and drive into the affluent neighborhoods of San Pasqual; "the Latino kids turn right and go into Laurel City."

San Pasqual High School brings together students from several local communities, including some very affluent neighborhoods as well as some of the most impoverished in California. Jenny and her family live somewhere in the middle, between cultures and languages and economies. Jenny has known extreme poverty, and she has witnessed her family's financial successes. She has a car and her own bedroom, and she receives fee waivers for all of her standardized tests and applications. When she goes to college, she will need significant financial aid; for the family of six, her parents' income for 2003 is just over $37,000. This perspective is unique and troubling: She looks out of the library window and recognizes something about affluence and something about poverty—and the distances from where she stands to each. She also recognizes the ways in which the world is divided by race and class. Out of the parking lot, she turns right.

We agree to meet in the late afternoon at her house; after school, she has soccer practice and won't arrive home until 4:30 or so. So before we part ways at the library, she draws me a map to her house. "You gotta drive a long way on Marina Road," she explains. "You'll see my stepdad's van in the drive-way . . . 'Ready Cleaners.'"

123 SMITH COURT EAST

I arrive at the scheduled time and ring the doorbell. A red Saturn is parked in the driveway next to a large black Cadillac Escalade and a white van with a business logo painted on the side in blue and red: "Ready Cleaners." The house is located on a quiet cul-de-sac in Laurel City, gray and white, with a small lawn strewn with children's toys. I stand at the door for what seems like several minutes until I hear small footsteps and the clinking of a turning knob. When the door opens, my eyes move down: Serena has opened the door. She is five years old and has large brown eyes, and she stares at me, say-ing nothing. "Hi," I say. "Is Jenny here?" Without responding, she runs off and begins yelling in Spanish. I keep standing in the doorway, straining to see through the mesh of the screen door.

Carlos, Jenny's stepdad, passes Serena in the hallway and comes to meet me. "I'm here to talk with Jenny," I start to explain. He shakes my hand and invites me into the house; he shows me to the couch and explains that Jenny is in the shower. She'll be out in a minute. Do I want anything to drink? No, I tell him, and settle into the couch. Marianna comes out of the kitchen fol-lowed by Tony and Carlos Jr. She sits down next to me and tries to talk as the boys wiggle around her. Serena turns somersaults and practices cartwheels; one of the boys knock into her and they all laugh. In the background, I can barely hear the shower over the sound of the "Power Puff Girls" playing on the large television.

FAMILY—PART I

Jenny is always surrounded by her extended family. Her grandfather takes care of the kids each day while Jenny's parents are working, and several of her aunts and uncles live in Laurel City. A few live a little farther away in Hawthorne and East Bayside. In addition to homework, Jenny's weekends are filled with family birthdays, baptisms, Quinceañeras, soccer games, and weddings. She often drives to Sacramento or Monterey with her family, visit-ing Carlos's relatives or checking business arrangements. Her biological father lives close by as well, about 20 minutes away, but she does not see him often. "His wife has a problem with me," she explains. "She didn't want me there." Now that her father and stepmother have a child of their own, Jenny has tried to keep in touch. "I want to be there for their daughter, you know. But it is hard. I don't think my stepmom has gotten used to me. But I'm like, 'what did I do?' I barely know her."

Each night, when Jenny arrives home from various practices and club meetings, she eats dinner with her family. "We always eat together, always. Well, unless I'm at school late or something." Two nights per week, Jenny has both soccer and volleyball practice, so she is rarely home before 9:00 P.M. "My mom, though, she comes and sits with me while I eat. It's superimportant, that she and I have time to just sit down and talk and everything. No matter how busy I am, or what is going on, we always sit together. That's really important." Jenny's mother comes up often in our conversations, starting from the first evening when we watched the Quinceañera video. Marianna is Jenny's "strength," her "motivation." Jenny remembers, "[my mom] says to me, 'you just be you,' so I check myself and, you know, remember what it's about . . . I know it was hard for her, and I know she made a lot of sacrifices to be successful. Now she's going to school and everything. I want to help her be the kind of person she wants to be. I help however I can." Sometimes this means getting up early in the morning to help her mom with homework before she goes to school. "I get up at 5:00, and my mom is in the kitchen doing her homework, English, and so I help her. I can't say no, even when I'm like so tired."

Jenny's house is always noisy and energetic. "It's the kids," Jenny says. They like to listen to Tejano music in the afternoons and dance. When Jenny sits down to do her homework, her brothers often come into her room and help. "Sometimes when I start my homework really late," she explains, "and I'm like so tired, Tony will come in and sit on the floor next to me, and it's just so great. [The kids] give me energy to stay awake and finish my homework." She gives them blank sheets of paper and they "do schoolwork" while Jenny works on her calculus. Carlos Jr. arranges himself on the floor and puts his chin in his free hand; he mimics Jenny as she thinks, tapping a crayon to his forehead. When the boys get tired, they get up on her bed and crawl under the covers. "They call it a sleepover," Jenny says. "They are so funny; they sleep forever! I get up in the morning, and there they are, at the end of the bed, all curled up together, still."

GREAT AMERICA

"This summer, I barely did anything . . . too busy working and everything.

But twice Alex [Jenny's boyfriend] and I took my sister and brothers to Great America. It was crazy, you know, because sometimes you see little kids and the parents are like walking and pushing them in strollers. Well Alex and me, we made them walk everywhere, like all over the park, from like 11:00 to 5:00. So they were so tired. We were walking to the car, and Alex had Carlos Jr. on his shoulders, and his head . . . I think he was sleeping, you know [gesturing with her hands] on his head. And then Tony was on my shoulders, and I was holding Serena's hand, and then Alex and I were holding hands, so we were like this little family. And people were really looking at us. I know they were like 'oh my gosh, look at that girl, she has all these kids!' And then Alex goes: 'do you see everyone looking at us?' And I'm like 'yeah.' But you know, Carlos Jr. and Tony used to call me "mommy" all the time—all the time. Serena, too. Tony and Carlos Jr. only started calling me 'Jenny' about three months ago. Isn't that funny?"

YENI GUTIERREZ

The email in my inbox is time-stamped 1:23 A.M. Jenny has sent me an early morning note:

> I just wanted to thank you for showing an interest in what I do at school and perhaps my future in academics. I will see you on Friday! We're meeting at 5:00, right? Oh, and I have been wondering for some time why you would want to know about me. Did college prep pick me or did Ms. Jimenez? I don't know. I was just wondering why not people that had better grades and such. If you can, answer these questions before Friday but if you can't then perhaps we can talk about it during dinner. Now I have to go do my Bio homework!

As a senior, Jenny's school schedule is hectic; she has no time for electives. Her fall courses include advanced placement (AP) biology, AP English, AP Spanish, AP calculus, psychology, and AVID (a college prep course). Her 7th period is MESA, another college prep course. She has already taken the SAT and received a 1320, and last year she took the AP exam in English composition; she received a score of 4. She will take the SAT II and hopes to do well; she knows these test scores are important for her college applications.

Jenny is an athlete—volleyball and soccer. During the fall, she practices volleyball two evenings a week, and soccer another two evenings. She also coaches a girls' team through her parish, five- to six-year-olds, on Wednesday afternoons. The girls call her "Coach #1" because they don't remember her name. "They are soooo crazy," Jenny tells me. "I mean, I love them, and they are so great. And the parents, they are nice. The girls just go out and give everything they have."

With college applications due just around the corner, Jenny starts to feel anxious. Ms. Jimenez, one of her teachers, reminds the students in her 7th period that financial aid paperwork is due soon. Technically, she is not the college counselor at the high school, but Ms. Jimenez advises MESA students about where and how to apply for college. The regular college counselor, Jenny explains, "is for the white kids." Ms. Jimenez works with the Latino/a students.

Jenny was completing her FAFSA form when she discovered that her birth certificate does not have her "real" name:

> Yeah, my birth certificate says one thing, and then my social security card says another. My school records are the only ones with "Jenny Acevedo." . . . My birth certificate says "Yeni Gutierrez"—that's Jenny, in Spanish, and Gutierrez is my dad's last name. I didn't know my dad's name was on it; I forgot about my dad for a second.

> Acevedo is on my social security card; that's my mom's name. This is so confusing! I didn't even know my birth certificate said "Yeni" until I barely checked. I had to go and fill out forms to get everything right.

BAD STOMACH

Now that Jenny is in AP calculus, she sometimes forgets algebra and geometry. As she prepares for the SAT II, she worries about the math she has forgotten. "Spanish will be easy," she tells me. "And the literature part, I think that will be hard. It's just hard, you know. I gotta do the math, too. And now I've got a bad stomach again . . ."

Jenny's stomach has been bothering her recently—an ulcer she developed a year earlier has reappeared. "Is it stress?" I ask. "Or something else?" "I don't know," she answers. "It's the same thing I had like a year ago, it was around Easter. The doctor says it's something like bacteria, and it keeps being made in my stomach. And stress, you know." She is taking lots of Zantac and drinking milk, and recently she stopped eating margarine. Last week when she went for a visit to UC Berkeley, she took her own food with her so that she could be sure to have something that wouldn't bother her stomach: Wheat Thins, carrots, and a little broiled chicken. When we get together to talk at a local Chinese restaurant, she orders plain white rice and green tea.

The Spanish SAT II exam has a listening section and students are asked to bring a cassette player. Jenny didn't know about the tape player, so she arrives at the test without the right equipment. "Yeah, not only was my stomach bad, but then I didn't have the tape player." A friend had an extra cassette player and let Jenny borrow it, which was a relief, but then they discovered that the batteries were dead. Another friend had some extra batteries—also dead. "There was this girl sitting in the front," Jenny plays with her rice as she tells the story, "I don't know who she is. She had some new batteries, and she heard us, like getting all panicked, and so she handed them back to me." Jenny pauses for a moment but then begins again: "God's thrown me over physically with this stomach, but he loves me, he does."

Jenny didn't finish the math section of the test, but she finished the literature section with time to spare. "What the heck is going on here," she thought to herself as she looked at the exam clock. She figured she'd finish math; it is her better subject. "I guess my reading skills have really improved," she tells me.

A few weeks later, Jenny finds out that she received a perfect score on the Spanish section. 800. Her other scores were also excellent: 690 in writing, 650 in math.

JENNY'S BIRTHDAY

For the first time in Jenny's 17 years, her biological father wants to throw her a birthday party. "Invite four or five of your friends," he tells her. Jenny isn't sure why he wants to do this; "maybe he wants to make up for things, or something." She hesitates in inviting her friends, and in the end decides just to invite Alex. A few of her cousins will attend, but no friends from school. "No drama," she says. "I don't want the party to be, you know, weird."

Alex is a year younger than Jenny; he's a junior at St. Ignatius High School, a small private Catholic school which he has attended since 1st grade. The first time we meet, he shakes my hand warmly and smiles; "Nice to meet you." He's wearing a baseball cap backwards, a hat I'll see him wearing several times over the year—always backwards. Since our introduction, he hugs me each time we meet, and again when I leave. Though he has just turned 16, he seems older. Maybe it's the school uniform he and his classmates wear: the required khaki pants and a crisp white button-down. When it is cold, they can wear jackets or sweatshirts in blue or green, the school's colors. Maybe he seems older because of his self-assuredness. He never retreats from my questions or avoids eye contact. As he tells me about his birthday present for Jenny, his brown eyes are bright, lively. He has picked out a teddy bear angel for her. It is white, soft, and has delicate wings.

A few weeks after the celebration at her father's house, Jenny shows me the pictures: Jenny and one of her cousins, who has a birthday at the same time, standing in front of a cake. The script of red icing says "Happy Birthday" in Spanish. Jenny sitting on a couch talking with another cousin. "That's my dad, over there," she points to another figure in the photograph with his back turned to the camera. Jenny with white icing all over her face—

her cousin pushed her into her cake. "I got strawberry up my nose!" she tells me. The last picture is a close-up of Jenny and Alex. She holds the photo to her chest and laughs, trying to describe what the picture shows. "Alex is looking at me with this, like, hella-funny look on his face, like he's so mad or whatever. And I'm kissing his cheek. I'm being all sweet and he gives me this look! When we got these pictures back, we laughed so hard."

Jenny collects the pictures, puts them back in their paper envelope, and replaces them in the box she keeps under her bed. "We're so corny," she tells me. "Alex and me, we keep all this stuff. I have a special box."

ALEX DESCRIBES JENNY

Unique. She's one of the smartest people I know. She knows what she wants. She is fair, she's honest, she has a good plan, she knows what she wants to do with her life.

FAMILY—PART II

Jenny has a great-uncle, who is 23, and an uncle, who is 22. "My great-grandmother and my mom were pregnant at about the same time—my mom was really young. And then my Tio, he was really jealous when I was born, 'cause he was just about five or something. But he was really an inspiration; he used to walk me to school. When we lived with him and my grandma, and we were really poor, my bike got stolen from our apartment. I was so sad, 'cause it was new and everything. But then at school, I saw two kids and they had my bike. So my Tio went and got it from them."

"Yeah, he tells me, 'cause he had some troubles in high school, he wants to go to Foothill [community college], and he's trying to get his education. I'm surprised I haven't talked about him before, because he's really important. He's like one of the reasons I want to go to college. The other day, he said to me: 'Hey, you talking about me to that lady?'"

IN-N-OUT BURGER

Jenny answered the door when I picked her up on Sunday afternoon. I could tell immediately that something wasn't right. She didn't have on any makeup, and her hair was pulled back in an awkward pony tail. "Can you wait about 15 minutes?" she asked. "I just need to talk to my mom." As I waited in the car, I wondered what was going on. Jenny was usually carefully dressed, with eye shadow to match her outfit and lip gloss freshly applied.

She walked out of her house about 30 minutes later carrying two heavy backpacks and a duffle bag. "Boy, do I have a lot to tell you," she started. "Can you take me to my dad's house after lunch?. . . . Let's go to In-n-Out."

In the car, Jenny continues: "I had to quit soccer at school. I mean, it's not just that my stomach is bothering me. I just feel like I owe it to myself to rest a little bit and spend time with my family. My brothers are really growing. I don't want to miss that. And I want to do more community service. When I get to college, I'm gonna have to go as hard as I can, you know, to do well. I want to rest a little now so that I can go really hard later.

"But since my birthday, I've been feeling like really bad. Just, you know, worn down. I need to get quiet or something. So I told my mom and my stepdad that I want to go to my dad's house for a few days, just to kind of relax, you know, do some homework. My mom got really worried just now, and she cried. She thinks I don't like it at home anymore, like it is too busy or something, the kids bothering me. They think that something happened while I was at my dad's house for my birthday, and now I'm different. But I'm like, how? I'm not different. So she's really mad at me, and Carlos is too. But I kept telling them—it's just for a few days. I'll come home on Tuesday. I don't know. It is so hard, I don't know what to say."

We sit in a red plastic booth at In-n-Out Burger for lunch, where Alex will meet us later—he can take Jenny to her father's house if that is what she wants to do. Though her father lives just 20 minutes away, Jenny doesn't spend much time with him. Partly this is because of his new wife, but also because Jenny is loyal to her stepfather and brothers and sister. When she talks about family, she always refers to her mother and stepfather, and the lively group of cousins and aunts that live nearby. Serena, Jenny's younger sister, doesn't know that they have different biological fathers. "Yeah," Jenny tells me, "she thinks Carlos is my real dad."

Over French fries and lemonade, Jenny talks about her conversation with her parents and her decision to stay with her biological father for a few days. Her eyes water. "It's just so much pressure," she says. "So much."

ALEX TELLS HOW HE MET JENNY—PART I

"How did we meet? We met at a house party, last April—like seven months ago. It was her friend's birthday, and my friend met her friend . . . well, it's really complicated. I knew her friend Edie, and Edie invited me to her party. So then I met her at that party. It was weird. I mean, the way we met. I barely got there, because I was at a Quinceañera that day, and it was really weird that my parents even let me go 'cause it was really late. It was like around nine. I told my parents I was gonna go over there to Laurel City, and I was over here, in Bayside, and that's a pretty long drive.

"Right when I got there, my friends, there was like a group of us, Julio, Tony, and Albert, and I was looking around just to see who was there, and I saw her. She was just like sitting down, and I see her look at me, and she said, 'You wanna dance?' I was like, 'All right.' I asked her for her number that day. I'm like, 'You're cool people and I want to get to know you.' But she was all 'Why don't you give me yours,' and I was like, 'Ah, shoot. She's not gonna call me. God, just my luck.' But I gave her my number. Like two or three days later, she called me, but I missed her call. And she said, 'Yeah, if you want to call me, leave a message with my friend so she can tell me if' . . . [*laughs*] yeah. So I called her friend, and her friend is like 'she really wants to talk to you.' So we finally talked, and we set up a date to go to the movies, with her friend. And then we went to the movies, and the movies was like really significant. I don't know. Like I felt like I knew her. Right away. You know, it's kind of weird. It was the three of us at the movies: me, Jenny, and her friend."

EMAIL EXCHANGE: JENNY IS SICK, AGAIN

December 3, 2003, 9:14 A.M.

Hi Jenny,

I hope you've had an un-stressful week. I just wanted to touch base with you about next week, (Friday). I'm planning to stop by and see you at 4. If that doesn't work for you, just let me know!

I look forward to seeing you again soon,

Julia

December 3, 2003, 10:31 P.M.

Hey Julia,

I actually have had a good week except for the fact that I got very very sick again but the favt that I had to catch up on two days of missed school actually motivated me alot and I even got ahead so that today I didnt have homweork and just relaxed with my family that came over to watch a soccer game. Oh! and friday the 12th is still good. .Alex is going to be with us right? if not then just let me know and I'll tell him plans have changed. You know what I wanna do? If Alex does come with us I'd kind of like ir for you to talk to him in private. I son;t know, I think he might say different things if I'm present then if I;m not.

Let me knoe what you think. Let me know what can happen and we'll keep in touch. Thank You!

Jenny

SPINAL TAP

All of Jenny's college applications have been sent, except Santa Clara University. When we meet, she lists them for me, ticking off the schools: the University of California campuses, the Cal State schools, the privates. Her list is extraordinarily long—14 in all—including schools she has no intention of attending. She applies for the status that admission brings; a tall stack of acceptance letters count as academic successes separate from grades and test scores. The letters will be individual victories, small details in a larger collage of achievement. She wonders if she should apply to some schools that have undergraduate majors in business.

"I probably want to stay somewhere up here for college. A friend of mine goes to Santa Clara, so that's like at the top of my list. I want to go to Berkeley, and it is close, so I would like do that and also come home a lot. But my mom, she wants me to go to Santa Clara—she knows it is my top choice, well, top choice with Berkeley. I don't think I could be much farther away than Berkeley; I want to be there for my family, for my brothers and sister."

She asks if I'll bring her some information about the business major at USC and she thinks about applying to Stanford. She has worked hard to raise her test scores and high school GPA so that she'll be a competitive candidate: 1330 on her SAT I; 800 (Spanish), 690 (writing), and 650 (math) on her SAT IIs; College Board National Hispanic Scholar, 3.5 GPA, five AP classes. But before she can complete any additional applications, she is sick again, and she ends up in the hospital. Her headache was so bad at the beginning of December, she had to get a spinal tap to rule out meningitis, and she missed a whole week of school, except Tuesday. She was feeling better, so she packed a blanket for herself and went to school, only to leave before the day's end. When I pick her up on Friday night, for our usual 4:00 appointment, her voice sounds terrible. She looks pale and tired; she has sick eyes.

"How I've been feeling," she tells me, "I was thinking, 'I've got all my UC and CSU applications in, and San Jose State,' and I'm like 'forget about the privates.' This is the first time I've heard her sound even remotely defeated. Usually she just plows through, calling everything a challenge and facing it with her eyes open. She's tired of being sick.

On Wednesday, Jenny's mom had a "breakdown." "Mija," she said, "how can I help you? Do you want me to take you to the hospital?" She was worried, Jenny tells me: "You know, she's like, 'How can I help my daughter?'" Her mom fixed some herbs, a cool cloth, and tied it to Jenny's forehead with a bandana. Jenny couldn't open her eyes because of the headache. When I saw her on Friday night, she told me it was the best she's been all week—"maybe in a long time." One day she was so bad, her mom said: "Do you want Alex? I'll go get him!"

Three days later I receive an email from Ms. Jimenez. She has sent a message to all of Jenny's teachers and advisors:

December 15, 2003

Hello all,

As you may know, Jenny has been out recently due to a series of medical issues. She had fluid extracted from her spine and then she contracted the flu. This week she will be out on Th and Fr for another procedure related to an ulcer.

She is under a tremendous amount of pain and fatigue. I believe she came to school today and is worried that she will not do well this semester due to these absences and circumstances.

I have spent time talking to her over the phone assuring her to stay positive and that she needs to focus on getting healthy and strong.

If there is anything you can do to help her, please do so. I have advised her to use the break to get back on track.

M. Jimenez

ALEX TELLS HOW HE MET JENNY—PART II

We got together on September 12. I was like really nervous, I was shaking. 'Cause I asked her parents like four weeks before that, and I'd only known her for two months I think. And then, you know, I called, and I asked her parents, I was like, "I want to know if I can go out with Jenny." And I remember her mom, saying, "Already?!" And I was like, "Oh no." I was like, "Shoot." And I got so nervous, and I asked her stepdad. And then he was Like, "You gotta come to us, personally, not on the phone." And I was like, "Oh, it doesn't get any worse." And then I asked them again about 2 or 4 weeks later, at a concert we all went to, and um, I don't know, but I remember one thing [Jenny] said. She's like, you know, she's working for her parents, you know, really hard, taking care of the kids, doing school work. And she said she's gonna work a lot more harder so that she can do all those kind of things and still spend time with me.

GASTROENTEROLOGY

"I went to the doctor again today," Jenny explains. "He says there is some kind of bacteria that keeps coming back to my stomach. I'm glad I'll have these two weeks off now [for Christmas break] 'cause I can rest. But it sucks because I can't eat anything. I'm like eating all this plain food, you know. And I have to go next week to see another doctor . . . I called today to make the appointment. Yeah, I make all my own doctor's appointments. It is where they put that camera down into your stomach. I felt really dumb because I had to practice the word on the card so I could say it when I called. Um, what is it? [*reaches into her purse and pulls out a business card*]. Gastro-enter-ologist. So I called, and I'm like: 'Hi, I need to schedule an appointment to see a gastroentrol . . .' Except I said it right."

AP SPANISH

As the bell rings to signal the beginning of period 4, students reach into backpacks and pull out books, magazines, and notebooks. The first 20 minutes of the period are dedicated to Sustained Silent Reading (SSR). Everyone reads. Jenny is reviewing her homework for calculus; she has a test later.

With the exception of one African American student, all of the 28 students in AP Spanish are Latino/a. They sit in two sections with an aisle down the middle, where Mr. Ramirez paces back and forth as they discuss the poetry. Today's text is "Canción de Jinete," a Federico García Lorca poem. Jenny is an active participant in the discussion. Spread out on her desk are several colored pencils, pens, and highlighters. She underlines the *metáfora* in red; the *personifacion* is in blue. When Mr. Ramirez asks the class about *elemento surrealista*, Jenny raises her hand and points to a particular line: "¡Qué perfume de flor de cuchillo!" "*Sí,*" her teacher answers. He glides down the aisle and points to another student.

When the class is over, Jenny places her notes in her three-ring binder. Her copy of the poem is beautiful, covered in multicolored printing, small and precise notes written next to the lines of poetry. It looks like a map, or a complex menu at a restaurant; she uses at least five different colors. At the top of the page, she has included a key.

WWW.EMODE.COM (ULTIMATE PERSONALITY TEST)

As an assignment in her psychology class, Jenny takes a personality test online. She summarizes her results:

Although I do not base my actions on what other people think, when I do something I expect to feel a personal reward and that people appreciate or recognize what I do. I do things in order to feel good about myself and then be of value to others, and I do feel that one of my biggest fears is not being good enough to meet my own expectations and other people's.

I do feel most happy and fulfilled when I finish something and demonstrate to others that I am capable of doing certain things. And when I say I can do something I do it.

HIGHLIGHTS

I arrive at Jenny's house on a Friday afternoon and find a note attached to her front door. The note, written in purple ink, is secured with a band-aid decorated with Muppet characters:

Hi Julia,

I hope you got my message but if you didn't, I'm at the Beauty Salon by Starbucks. The stylist said he'd be done by 3:30. You can wait for me here or just go pick me up there. Call me when you get here.

—Jenny

"The Montel Williams" show is playing on the overhead TV as I walk into the salon. I am carrying a cup of coffee for myself and a vanilla frappuccino for Jenny—she can't have caffeine still because of her stomach. She is sitting in a dryer chair, her hair wrapped in little strips of tin foil, and she is reading a magazine. When she sees me, she smiles and says: "You're seeing me as very few people have!"

While her hair dries and the color sets, she tells me about her weekend plans: a Quinceañera, homework, maybe a movie with her younger brothers. She is looking forward to the Quinceañera party because she likes to dance. "It's cool," she tells me, "because Alex is a really good dancer. We teach each other; he's good at house dancing. Yep, he's my dancing partner." It is fortunate that Alex is an enthusiastic dance partner, she continues: "If you don't like to dance, then no. I wouldn't want to be with a person that wouldn't want me to dance."

Jenny's stylist takes the foil out of her hair and examines the highlights. "Good color," he says. "I'm talented." Ricardo has always done Jenny's hair. He did her hair for her Quinceañera—piled on top of her head with ringlets of curls—and for all of her school dances. She will come back next week so that he can do her hair for the Valentine's Dance at school. After Ricardo finishes drying her hair, he shows her how he will style it for the dance. "See, pulled back like this. Maybe with bangs."

FALL SEMESTER GRADES

Economics	B+
AP Calculus	B
AP English	D
AP Spanish	A
AP Biology	B
Pyschology	A
AVID	A

Sick and out of school at the end of the first semester, Jenny fell behind and could not catch up. "I got a D in AP English," she tells me, "but it's like: that's not my grade." She is not used to receiving grades lower than A's and B's—she only has three B's on her high school transcript. "I just couldn't turn in a really big assignment. But my teacher knows that that's not my usual grade. She's gonna write a letter to the [Berkeley] Incentive Award people, and my bio teacher too. I'm gonna ask Ms. Hong to write a letter too, maybe Ms. Jimenez. I just don't know what else to do."

COLLEGE CHOICE—PART I

By the middle of February, college acceptances begin to arrive. And with good news, Jenny's health also returns: She feels well enough to play league soccer in her community; she can eat carnitas again. Brown has offered Jenny a spot in the 2004–2005 freshman class, and Notre Dame (located in Belmont, California) offered admission and a substantial scholarship. "I wasn't even happy about Notre Dame," she admits. "I mean, it's nice, but, you know, it's not like getting into Berkeley." Jenny called Alex to tell him about Brown, and he responded enthusiastically, announcing to the rest of his track team: "My baby got accepted into Brown!" "I was embarrassed," Jenny tells me, "and I wasn't even there." She also learned about a $500 scholarship awarded through a community organization, and she received some financial aid from the Hispanic Scholarship Fund. In the next week, a representative from Brown would come to Laurel City to talk with Jenny about financial aid and scholarships. "But I'm not going to Brown," she admits. "It is in Rhode Island—too far away."

In the kitchen of her house, Jenny tells her mother that she was admitted to Brown. "But she didn't really react," Jenny remembered. "I don't think she really understands, you know, that it's a big deal. She was washing dishes or something."

Jenny's first choice is Berkeley, especially if she gets the "Incentive Award." But she is nervous. "Last year, some people got into Harvard, but not to Berkeley. So many people didn't get in last year. I guess if I don't go there, my second choice is Santa Clara. [Santa Clara] is big, but not too big, and it is pretty. I can see myself there, you know, walking there. That's where my friend David is at. And I want to be somewhere with a normal social life." For now, she just waits. She should hear from Berkeley at the end of March.

SOCCER PRACTICE: ANOTHER INJURY

Jenny comes to the front door of her house on crutches.

> Last week, we had soccer practice [for the community league], and I was running down the field. I thought I felt something, you know, kind of twist or something, but I just kept going. I hate missing practice, and we were almost done for the day. And then the next day I went to a party at my aunt's house, and danced all night long. There was like this circle of people around me, dancing. My uncles are really good dancers too. They teach me new steps. And then Sunday when I got up, I was like, 'Oh, no, that's not right . . .' I finally went to the doctor on Wednesday, and there's like fluid in my knee; it's like swollen. So now I have to stay off of it for a couple of days and see what happens. Geez. I just get healthy, and then this happens. I've already got bruises on my hands from using these crutches. See? Look . . . right here.

THE JEANNE S. DICKEY AWARD

The Family Service Agency of Woodland County hosts an annual awards breakfast for local students. The program begins:

> *There are academic honors for scholars*
> *And banners for athletic champions,*
> *But many remarkable heroes go unnoticed.*
> *Family Service Agency of Woodland County brings together local businesses, school*
> *districts and community leaders to honor a group of true winners.*
> *They are graduating seniors from schools throughout the county who have*
> *succeeded in spite of significant obstacles.*
> *Their stories will inspire you.*

Ms. Jimenez has nominated Jenny for the award, which includes a five-hundred-dollar scholarship. Someone from the agency came to her school and took her picture for the program. The photograph shows her standing in front of one of the school buildings with her backpack on; her long dark hair is pulled back into a ponytail.

The program includes a full page for Jenny and all of the other award winners. Her award, her picture too, come first in the program booklet. At the top of the page, just above her picture, is the heading: "The Winners." Ms. Vasquez submitted the description of her background and academic and extracurricular talents. "Jenny has excelled in academics, sports and extracurricular activities. She's taken advanced placement and honors classes, demonstrates fine leadership skills and is conscientious and sympathetic to others. She speaks and writes very well and is a positive role model for other young Latinas who want to pursue higher education."

When we talk about the awards ceremony over breakfast at Denny's, Jenny remembers the other winners and talks about their hardships: students living in foster homes, students with learning disabilities, gang members, teen parents, abusive families, and severe illness. She pauses, looks down at her plate, and says: "I mean, wow, it's like hearing their stories, I'm like, 'I don't belong with this group. In comparison, I have it so easy.'"

ADMISSION LETTERS

By the middle of March, Jenny has received 13 letters of acceptance:

Brown
Santa Clara
University of California, Davis
University of California, Santa Barbara
University of California, San Diego
Cal Poly, San Louis Obispo
San Diego State
San Jose State
Chico State
University of San Francisco
California State University, Hayward
California State University, Dominguez Hills
Notre Dame

Along with acceptance letters come offers of scholarships and grants. Jenny compiles them, adding the figures in her head and marveling at the large number. "Notre Dame is like giving me $48,000. I mean, I'm not gonna go there, but whoa." After a stressful fall, full of illness and exams, Jenny gathers the admission letters, treating each with subtle reverence. Her pile of acceptances do not represent an impending choice—she already knows, has known, where she will go to college: Berkeley or Santa Clara. Instead, they are markers of her success and hard work which she will stack neatly in a memory box under her bed.

Despite all the good news, Jenny is still anxious. When she checks the on-line admission system at UC Berkeley, her file is still marked: "pending."

NEIGHBORHOOD CHICKEN

Jenny and I drive up to her house after dinner on a Friday evening, and there is a chicken digging around on the front lawn. At first I don't notice it; it is twilight and darkening. But Jenny's reaction points my attention to the far end of the lawn. "Oh my god," Jenny says. "That chicken. I can't get out of the car yet." Jenny is profoundly afraid of birds, including chickens. She explains: "But only live chickens; I like chicken, you know, to eat." While we wait for the chicken to move on, out of the yard, Jenny tells me about another chicken encounter:

> See, the chicken lives next door, or right there in that house. But I didn't know it was there. One day I came driving home, and I looked in the rearview mirror, and there was this chicken. And I was like [she puts her hands over her eyes] "I'm hallucinating!" And then I looked again, and it was still there, so I turned around, and sure enough, this chicken was just standing there. I was like, "Oh no!" I put my backpack on in the car and ran into the house. I couldn't look at it.

When the neighborhood chicken sets off across the sidewalk and toward the end of the cul-de-sac, Jenny braces herself to leap from the car and run inside. As she grabs the handle, however, she stops to ask a question. "Oh yeah," she says, "I was wondering, um, like my friend asked me what, you know, you're doing. Like what your job is. What should I tell him?"

EMAIL FROM JENNY: SENIOR PROJECT
AND NEWS FROM UC BERKELEY

March 30, 2004, 6:29 P.M.

Hi Julia,

I was just about to write to you. Remember that Senior Exhibition Project I told u about? the one that all seniors have to do and if we don't there's a huge chance we don't graduate. Well, we're supposed to have our paper read my an adult editor . . . and mine backed out at the last minute. Sooo I was hoping that u could do me a huge favor and be my editor. It s due on friday and my teachers are all booked up with other students so I have nobody else. Do you htink if I send you a copy by tingight that you could have it edited by thrusday afternoon? That is if you're ot to busy to look at it. Yeah friday would be good to meet. Maybe it would be goof if you could come over her tomorrow or thursday? Call me or write back to me a.s.a.p tog see what gonna happen. Thank a lot Julia. . Oh and I haven't heard from berkeley yet. I'm waiting.

Jenny

March 31, 2004, 3:52 P.M.

Oh my god Julia,

Than you sooo much. I'll send you the draft tonight so hopefully I can get it back on thursday night. Is there a faxumber I can send you thing to? There is an editing page in which yo uhave to fill out some questions so It 'd be good to get those to you at the same time as the draft. call me or write me back. thanx a lot. oh and i got into berkeley but i din't get the incentive. but it's okay because i already talked to some people and they are willing to help me withj scholarships, yeah, people from organizations at berekeley. talk 2 u 18r.

Jenny

April 1, 2004, 1:39 A.M.

Hey Julia,

Sorry for not sending my draft earlier but I had tons of homework and I took my medicine for my knee pain and it knocked me out so I took a forced nap. I faxed u two papers. One is like a letter on which u have ot fill out ur name and stuff, and the other is actually where you have to evaluate me. Thank you so uch again, u saved me! I thought that it would be best to send my draft by e-mail becaus eotherwise it would've been an extremely long fax. So here I attahced my draft. Thank you and I'll be waiting to hear from you tomorrow afternoon. Thanx a lot Julia.

MARGINALIA

I have to read Jenny's e-mail twice, then again. She got into Berkeley. I'm not surprised by the news—I know Jenny is a great candidate—but I am surprised by the seeming nonchalance of her email. A year of anticipation boiled down to a sentence that begins: "oh . . ." I called as soon as I got her email:

Hi Jenny, I got your email, and I'll look at your paper tomorrow morning. And I'm soooo happy for you! Congratulations on getting into Berkeley. That's so great. I can't wait to hear all about it next week. See you later.

SPREADING THE NEWS ABOUT BERKELEY: APRIL FOOLS

"I called Ms. Jimenez first. Well, I got the incentive award information on the 31st, that I didn't get the award. Or, actually, I got the letter that I'm the first alternate, you know, in the mail. The girl that got the incentive award, she's Peruvian, but she's pretty much White. She didn't get into UCLA. I don't know, her GPA is like 4.3, but I think her SATs are low. She made a comment about me getting into Brown, like 'how did you get into Brown?' She's the valedictorian.

"Ms. Jimenez, she told me to call her as soon as I found out about Berkeley. I called her on her cell, and I pretended at first like I was all sad. I was like [in a flat tone] 'Hi Ms. Vasquez. I wanted to let you know about Berkeley . . . [now enthusiastically] I got in!' She was so mad at me, you know, for playing like I didn't get in. Then, I called Alex."

FAMILY REACTIONS

When her mom got home from work, Jenny rushed into the kitchen to tell her the news about Berkeley. "I told her, and she just walked away from me. She didn't say anything, she just went back to cutting carrots or whatever. And I was so sad, because my mom wasn't happy for me. It was like Brown all over again." Later that evening, she told Carlos the good news: "He gave me a big hug; I think he understands that it is a big deal. But he didn't really say, like, congratulations." Her biological father's response was probably the most blunt. He said: "Don't go there." When Jenny and I met to talk a few days later, she was still frustrated. "Geez," she said, "neither of my parents are happy for me. It's like I've done all this work, and nothing, you know? . . . Next week, my mom and I are going to go to school to meet with Ms. Jimenez to talk about it; my mom just doesn't understand about, you know, that Berkeley is a really good school. She thinks that Santa Clara is a better school because it is private."

COLLEGE CHOICE—PART II

Just after Easter weekend, Jenny leaves a message on my answering machine. Her voice sounds tired, defeated:

> Hi Julia. It's Jenny. I was just calling to see when you might be coming here again; I don't think we made plans last time. Um, I made a decision, to go to Santa Clara, and I guess I wanted to talk to you about that, get your advice. So if you could call me, that'd be great.

STREET SIGNS: SEARCHING FOR SANTA CLARA UNIVERSITY

Though it is only May, spring by all accounts, the afternoon is hot. Jenny and I are driving down the freeway with the air conditioning on. We're looking for Santa Clara University, and neither of us knows where, exactly, it is located. Jenny has been admitted and plans to attend, but she has never really visited the campus. We talk in the car about her decision.

"I haven't really told Ms. Jimenez and Ms. Hong yet. I mean, I talked to them about it, about Santa Clara, but they are disappointed, I know. They really want me to go to Berkeley. Ms. Vasquez was like, 'You know, you need to think about it.' I was supposed to go and talk to her about it after school today, but I just, I don't know."

"Why do you think they are disappointed?" I ask. "Why do they want you to go to Berkeley so badly?"

"Hmm. I don't know. I mean, I know it's a good school and everything. And I know that it means a lot that I got in, and you know . . . being Latina. And they really helped me out to get in there. Ms. Vasquez asked me, she thinks maybe I want to go to Santa Clara because of Alex, because it's closer to him. And closer to my family. But I'm like, 'No.' I'm gonna be busy, I'm not gonna be seeing Alex all the time, I'm not gonna be going home all the time. I mean, yeah, I want to be close to my family. That's important. But that's not why I want to go to Santa Clara."

A freeway sign advises that we are close to campus: "Santa Clara University next right." So we move into the next lane and follow the off-ramp. Palm trees line the street, but there is no sign of the campus. And no street signs. "I think you go right here," Jenny tells me. I complete the turn and ask: "What does Alex think about you going to Santa Clara?"

"He's cool. He knows I'm not leaving, leaving. Like I'm not leaving him, you know, wherever I go to school. If I go to Berkeley it's the same thing; I'm not *leaving*, I'm going to college."

Finally we see a street sign posted on a light pole. "Santa Clara University," and an arrow pointing to the right. Up ahead is the main gate: a wide street, lined with palm trees, leads to an information kiosk, where a parking attendant hands us a campus map and points behind him. "Guest parking is up there," he says, "two hours." We walk across a grassy quad toward the center of campus. The area is quiet; there are no students around though we can hear a radio somewhere in the distance. Everywhere we look there are brick buildings and green grass. At the student union, tables are set up advertising various campus organizations, and there's a coffee stand to our left. We stop for a snack. "Is that cheesecake?" Jenny asks the woman behind the counter. When the woman nods "yes," Jenny beams.

COLLEGE CHOICE—PART III

"I'm going to Berkeley." Jenny told me over the phone, just a few days after she submitted a deposit that would secure her place in the freshman class. The week before, we had wandered the grassy quad at Santa Clara with diet cokes and cheesecake. She explained:

> Well, I really stopped to think about why I wanted to go to Santa Clara, and like what I hoped to get out of it. I was thinking about all the things I want to do, like community service and everything, and Berkeley will be able to give me that, you know, much more. It's a bigger campus, and I'll have to really, like get involved in things. Santa Clara was just safer, and you know, I know I can do good there. Berkeley's gonna be just more.

Jenny is excited as she talks. She's clearly rehearsed these lines, thought about it a lot, and worried over how to explain her decision. "I mean, I'm glad we went and visited the campus and everything, you know? It's just, I think I need something, like a bigger community." Her teachers are happy, she tells me, and proud. And her family? "Yeah," she says, "I think my mom understands. I mean, like she's really happy. We had a big party, my mom made carnitas, and everyone came over; we danced till like, so late. The kids, though, I don't think they understand. They don't really know I'll be, you know, not living here."

AT THE TAQUERIA: SOCCER
AND ADVANCED PLACEMENT EXAMS

The restaurant is nearly empty—it is not yet 5:00 P.M. on a Friday evening. A television in the next room is tuned to the soccer game, and a young man sits at a table, talking excitedly to the players. Jenny and I stand for a long time in front of the counter, trying to decide what to order: fajitas, tacos, all sorts of enchiladas. "I'm starving," Jenny announces. "You're not gonna to believe what I'm ordering." We gather our drinks and take a seat near the young man, Jenny sitting so that she can see the television. Her favorite team is playing, and she wants to watch the action. The woman from behind the counter brings the chips and salsa Jenny has ordered. While she snacks, she tells me about her AP exams.

"Yeah, the APs. I took English, Spanish, and Calculus. At the ten minute break during the English test, I don't know if you remember, but we get a break between the sections. Everyone was like getting up and walking around. But I was, I don't know. I was okay just sitting. I wrote a poem for my mom for mother's day."

"A poem? During your break?"

"Uh huh. You know, you get that sheet of labels, the labels you use to like keep the booklet closed when you're done? I wrote the poem on that sheet. Just wrote it, I didn't really think about it. And I folded it and put it in my backpack. And then I took the rest of the test. I think [the poem] was easy to write because I've been reading so much lately, you know, to get ready for the tests and school and everything. The next day I rewrote it on notebook paper, and I was so surprised; it was really long, like two pages. I gave it to my mom on Sunday, everyone was over at our house for mother's day. And they made me read it out loud."

"How did you feel about your English exam?" I ask.

"Well, the last essay was rushed, but I think I did okay, maybe I got a 4. But the multiple choice was perfect. I was so surprised, because I knew everything. I wasn't expecting the multiple choice to be the easy part."

As Jenny talks, her eyes wander to the television screen. "Whoa," she says, and in the background I hear the broadcaster's voice rise. Jenny and the young man seated near us exchange exclamations—"Did you see that?" she asks him. "Geez, barely made it." The other team has threatened to score. I turn around in my seat in time to see the instant replay; the soccer ball sails over the goalie, just inches too high. No goal. Even though they've already seen the near goal, Jenny and the young man are as animated during the replay as when they watched it in real time. The waitress stops at our table and delivers my burrito.

"The Spanish AP was tricky," Jenny continues, still picking at her chips and salsa. "I mean, I think I was ready because it's like taking the English AP, but in Spanish, but it's funny because some of the terms in Spanish are different than in English. You know how you have to know the, like, things like rhyme scheme and stuff? Well in Spanish, some of the terms don't mean the same thing. Like 'consonance.' In Spanish, it means perfect rhyme, but in English, it means, um, alliteration with consonants. It's similar, but not really the same."

The waitress returns to our table with Jenny's order: mixed fajitas (chicken, beef, and shrimp) with flour tortillas, and a shrimp tostada. "See, this is a lot of food," Jenny says as she unwraps her tortillas from their aluminum foil. "I told you I was hungry!"

There's another near goal in the background, and Jenny's eyes return to the game. "That was close," she says. Eyes still following the soccer game, she wipes her fingers on a napkin and places it in the middle of her half-eaten plate of fajitas, which she then pushes to the center of the table. "Oh, I'm so full," she says, and her words are interrupted by a hiccup. "That's how I can tell I'm full, when I get the hiccups."

TIME FOR A CHANGE

The parking lot is already full when I arrive at San Pasqual High School. I'm directed to a grassy field on the other side of the school—closer to the football stadium, it turns out, than the regular student/faculty lot. As I turn a corner nearing the visitor seating area, I come upon the lineup of San Pasqual graduates: male students in orange caps and gowns, female students in white. In the distance, an arc of balloons—also white and orange—stretches across the middle of the field. The procession of graduates will walk along the track encircling the field, then under the arc of balloons, and into the white plastic chairs arranged in two large blocks. With the band playing "Pomp and Circumstance," and graduates filing across the field with carefully choreographed steps, I search for a place to stand. Every seat in the bleachers is taken.

Jenny and her family have been preparing for this day for several weeks. Invitations to Jenny's party have been printed and handed out; a family friend has been hired to make tacos on an outdoor propane grill; Marianna has purchased stacks of plastic cups and salsa bowls. Jenny's gown is carefully ironed and her cords—for CSF and MESA—are laid out, ready to wear. The house has even been rearranged: The family room furniture—including the large screen television—has been moved into the area just beyond the kitchen, and the dining furniture has been moved to the family room area. "We wanted a change," Jenny explained. "Doesn't it look great?" Alex laughs and looks around the room. "Do you know how heavy those things are?" he says, pointing to a set of cabinets with glass doors which have been moved to the far corner of the room. "I had to move them."

Graduation morning is cool and crisp, but it will soon be hot on the field, and the students are seated without a canopy to shield them from the sun. Jenny sits in the second row, which means she will be among the last to walk across the stage. She wears her MESA cord, a multicolored sash actually, with her bright yellow satin CSF cord laid over the top. Her hair is carefully secured under her hat, and she wears sunglasses to protect her eyes from the sunlight. "This is our time," the first student speaker begins. While he continues—"the future is whatever we make of it"—I scan the stands looking for Jenny's family. Finally, I spot them, and I quickly wonder what has taken me so long: They are all wearing white t-shirts with a silk-screened picture of Jenny in her cap and gown; across the top is written "Congratulations Jenny!" Marianna, Serena, Jenny's grandmother, Carlos Jr. and Tony, Alex, Alex's sister and brother, Jenny's cousin: All are wearing the shirts in various sizes. Alex holds a bouquet of helium balloons to the side, trying to keep them out of the sightlines of guests sitting behind him.

The t-shirts are a surprise, something Marianna organized. So when Jenny's name is called, and she walks up to the stage to shake hands, she is startled by the Jenny-t-shirt-clad group. From where I'm standing in the back, I watch Jenny hesitate after she receives her diploma, her eyes traveling up into the stands to where the shouts are coming from. "I was soooo surprised," she tells me later. "I had no idea. I was like. "how did my mom do that?'" Jenny smiles, then waves to her family and raises her diploma in her left hand. The extended family, still standing, cheers long after Jenny leaves the stage and settles back into her seat.

GRADUATION PARTY: BALLOONS AND STRAWBERRY MUSTACHES

When I arrive at the house a few hours after graduation, everyone is working. Jenny, her cousin Theresa, Alex (still wearing the Jenny t-shirt), and I are put in charge of decorating the backyard with orange and white balloons. The wind blows the balloons around, making it difficult to secure them around the patio. We try a few different configurations: tied to chairs around the large tables, taped to the tall fence at intervals. "It's too windy," Jenny announces, laughing. "We can't put them at the table. People will have balloons right in their faces. Let's just put them on the fence, and then in the frontyard, so people will know where the party is." Theresa and I hold the balloon bouquets—Marianna has purchased two dozen—while Alex and Jenny tape them to the fence. "You gotta take off that shirt," Jenny tells Alex while they work. And then to Theresa and me: "We were at the store, and people were like, uh, looking at Alex's shirt, and then at me, and they were like, 'Is that you?'" Jenny moves her head to one side, eyes in a suspicious squint, then to the other, mimicking the look and movements of the other shoppers. "I was like, 'Oh my God!'"

When the backyard is sufficiently decorated, we all move to the front driveway and begin tying the remaining balloons to the car port. Alex climbs up onto the "Ready Cleaners" van in order to reach the edge of the roof, then moves over to the opposite side and stands on the family car. Jenny and Theresa provide directions for balloon placement. "Aquí?" Alex asks, holding an orange and a white balloon over his head. "Sí," Jenny says "No," Theresa says. Alex moves the balloons about 2 feet to the right. "Aquí?"

The house is bustling with activity; Marianna and Jenny's grandmother are stirring large pots in the kitchen as the stereo sounds loudly in the background. Cholo, the family dog, keeps escaping out the back gate and running down the street. Each time he makes his escape, a chorus of children's voices calls out: "Cholo has escaped! Alex, go get Cholo!" Alex has been assigned the task of chasing him down when he runs into the neighbor's yard. As he dashes out the door, again in pursuit of the escaped dog, he yells: "It's a good thing I'm on the track team . . ."

One of Jenny's male cousins cuts cilantro, and Serena, wanting to help with the arrangements, pours "Pace" picante sauce into bowls. In the backyard, the taco chef begins heating the oil in the deep pan he'll use to fry the tortillas for taco shells. "He's a friend of my mom's," Jenny explains; "he comes from the same town in Mexico, and he makes the *best* tacos." Suddenly, Alex turns to me and says: "Where are all the balloons?" We look at one another, then at the fence where they had been placed. The wind was too strong and the tape was too weak. "Oh no," he says. "They're gone." And we all, including Jenny, laugh.

When the guests begin arriving, Jenny takes off the ballet-slipper like shoes she has been wearing and puts on tall, strappy black sandals. Her party shoes are much too uncomfortable for running around and decorating. Carlos empties a bag of ice into a tub of soft drinks in 2-liter bottles, and immediately, the kids swarm to the tub asking for strawberry soda. Tony, Carlos Jr., and Andre take plastic cups and fill them with ice, tiny hands in the large tub. They compete to see who can find the biggest chunk of ice and squeeze it into the cup. Because Andre is a few years older than the twins (4 1/2 years old), he decides to take charge of the soda bottle. He puts the cup of ice in the crook of his elbow and holds the bottle with his now-free left hand. Carlos Jr. and Tony stand by expectantly, eyes glued to the pink soda. With his right hand, Andre turns the cap without any luck. The bottle will not open. Jenny and I have been watching the boys in their soda pursuit, so she calls them over, opens the bottle, and pours a small amount in each boy's glass. "Gracias," the boys say as they run back to their seats. They are content, with pink mustaches, chatting and eating chips and salsa.

"They are so funny," Jenny tells me. "I was gonna get a job this summer, but then my mom said I could baby-sit the kids instead while she's at work. Give my grandpa a rest for a while. And you know, I was thinking, I'm gonna be gone real soon, so I'd like to spend time with the kids. We can go to the park, go swimming. I want to really spend time with them before I go."

EXPLODING PROPANE

The fire under the pot of oil is starting to bubble as Marianna comes out onto the patio. "Everything is nearly ready," she tells everyone. "We're just waiting for the tacos." A group of Jenny's high school friends are seated at one end of a long table, and Alex's parents at the other. I'm sitting across the table from Alex, and we're talking with Jenny's aunt and uncle. Suddenly, we hear a loud "pop" from the propane tank. But it's more than a pop—it's louder than that. Everyone seated close to the taco stand gets up in one motion; someone screams. Chairs scrape on the concrete patio as friends and family members run toward the patio door. Marianna grabs Carlos Jr. and Tony. Cholo runs into the house.

The only party guest who seems un-phased by the sudden propane explosion is the taco chef. He doesn't even move when it pops. Instead, he reaches over and shuts off the gas. While everyone scuttles around in a panic, he fingers the tubing and sees the hole. There's a rip in the tubing about half-way between the tank and the flame. I glance at Jenny, and she has her left hand over her mouth. "Ah, no," she says. "I'm so hungry for the tacos." "AAAleeeexx," Serena yells as she runs from inside the house. "Cholo is out! Run!" Alex doesn't disappoint, but says his exit line—"It's a good thing I'm on the track team"—and takes off in search of the dog.

PACKING LIST

In two weeks, Jenny will move into Clark Kerr Residence Hall to start her first year at UC Berkeley. Over Starbucks lattes, we talk about her packing list. "What will you bring with you?" I ask.

"A laptop" so that "everywhere can be my desk," she begins. "Shower sandals, definitely. Extra-long bed sheets. Isn't that funny? I mean, what am I gonna do with an extra long bed? I'm short! And I gotta go out and buy them, like I don't know where. It's like a joke!" We laugh together, then Jenny takes a deep breath. "Um," she continues, "my angels, I will definitely take my angels—you remember them, they're on my dresser?" I nod and she goes on: "Oh, my big Scooby Doo, and the rosary I got from my mom and my aunt for my Quinceañera, um, and the picture of my grandparents when they got married—'cause I look just like [my grandma]—uh, and I have a frame, maybe you saw it, it has like a poem on it. It's from my aunt. It goes like:

be nice, don't be easy
be sweet, not saccharine
be independent, not selfish
giggle, but don't laugh out loud.

Or something. They're like written around the edges of the frame, you know?" Jenny traces the edges in the air with both hands, then with her hands still raised in front of her: "I think I'm always between these, you know, like between independent and not selfish and everything. It's like a fine line; once you cross it, you gotta know you've passed it."

"But I'm not gonna take my memory boxes." As she talks I remember the box she keeps under the bed, full of pictures and movie stubs, letters of acceptance from colleges and greeting cards. "I have four of them now, three just for me and Alex. One for the flowers; I even save them when he just gives me one, like he picked it out of the yard on the way over. I'm about the small things, you know, little details."

"Yeah," she says, smiling, looking over my shoulder. "I'm gonna keep those boxes at home. I gotta get new boxes."

5

....

Paz M. Olivérez

Urban Students, Social Ecologies—Part II

...

THE CAMPUS

One day I arrive between class periods. The halls are packed with students. It is obvious to the onlooker that Esperanza's student population is primarily Latino, 89% to be exact, with the second largest group being Asian students (5%). Data collected by the school state that 2% of the student population is made up of African Americans and less than 1% of white students. School-collected numbers indicate that Esperanza students come from over 40 countries and speak over 20 different languages. Among their countries of origin are Mexico, El Salvador, Guatemala, China, Thailand, Cambodia, Korea, the Philippines, and several other Central American, Asian, and African nations. Spanish is reported by 88% of Esperanza's students as their home language, while others speak Korean, Chinese, Tagalog, and several additional languages. Ninety-five percent of Esperanza's students have acquired English as their second language.

During each break, students rush from one end of the sprawling campus to the other, trying to avoid getting caught in the "tardy sweep." The unfortunate students who are found in the halls after the bell rings are taken to the "tardy sweep" room, where they sit for the entire period, thus missing out on the instruction they would have received if they had arrived to class on time. Other students stand near their lockers chatting with friends or push their way through the sea of students. I make my way up the stairs to the second floor of the four-story main school building, trying to go with the flow of traffic and making an effort not to get trampled by the boisterous crowd of students pouring downstairs in the opposite direction. When I get to the second floor, I walk past classrooms, the student cafeteria, a few administrators' offices, and finally arrive at Esperanza's college office.

THE COLLEGE OFFICE

Walking into this cramped 10 by 25 foot room, I am struck by the fact that the staff must do so much with so little. On several occasions I have walked into the college office to find it crowded with Esperanza students and counselors trying to gather or distribute college-related information, highlighting its centrality to helping students get much-needed college preparation. Recruiters from various local colleges and universities also use this space to meet with students who are potential college-goers and/or part of university-sponsored outreach programs. On most days, particularly around college and financial aid application deadlines, the office is bustling with activity. Typically there are two to four "service" students working in the office each class period who help the college counselor with odd jobs such as filing, summoning students to the college office, and assisting with college-related activities. Students receive graduation, but not college, credit for doing "service" at school. The students whom I have observed using the college office most often are Latina and Asian females. However, some male students from both groups visit the office as well.

On this morning I walk in to find three students sitting at the one narrow table in the room talking to Ruby, an undergraduate college student and recruiter from a local state college. With four people sitting around the table, the room is already crowded. I squeeze pass them and one of the two computers in the room to find Josie, the assistant to Mr. Bowman, Esperanza's one college counselor. Mr. Bowman is not around—he is an army reservist and has been called to active duty as a result of the war in Iraq—leaving Josie, a college student herself, and another part-time employee, responsible for running the office. Josie is a tall, thin, mild-mannered Latina, with straight, dark-brown hair cut short, just below her ears. She is a former Esperanza student and fluent in both English and Spanish, and she was one of the first people I got to know when I began visiting the campus. With her assistance, I was able to gain entrée into many spaces. During our first formal interview, she was helpful in suggesting other people and places I should be sure to see in order to gain greater insight into everyday life at Esperanza.

During this first meeting and on several occasions since, Josie has expressed her frustration with the school administration's lack of attention to their requests for more space and resources. She discusses her dismay with the lack of support and explains that she and Mr. Bowman have been fighting for more space for years. On any given day, 30 or more students may visit the college office. Some may visit briefly to get a scholarship or fee waiver application, whereas others may need to sit down with the counselor to make sure their courses meet college requirements. In any case, at a school with over 5,000 students, almost 700 of them seniors, giving all students the necessary attention to ensure their preparation for college is impossible. Mr. Bowman, the students, and their parents have gone to the principal and other administrators to plead for more resources, but there is little response despite the principal's charge to students that more of them ought to be going to college. The dearth of support for those in the college office does little to improve Esperanza's already dismal graduation and college-going rates, which are 48% and 45%, respectively. Because of these low numbers, educationally savvy parents who desire for their children to go on to college will often find ways to transfer their children to high schools in the more affluent San Fernando Valley or have them attend more specialized magnet high schools within the district. This reality not only compromises the quality of education offered at Esperanza High School, but it also negatively impacts the level of expectations of Esperanza students by teachers and administrators.

After a brief conversation with Josie, I inquire about a Salvadoran student named Laura. Some weeks earlier, I had observed Laura in her classes, and I wondered about the progress of her college applications. While sitting in her homeroom, Laura explained that she had participated in a college preparatory program at UC Berkeley and hoped she would be able to go there for college. Josie informed me that Laura had been accepted and would indeed be starting at UC Berkeley in the fall of 2004. Laura was a shy, but very driven young woman who received little academic support at home. When we spoke, she explained that her mother was pleased that she was doing well in school but knew little about Laura's role as drum line leader, leadership secretary, and advanced placement student—just a few of the things that Laura was doing to ensure that she would get into the college of her choice.

Laura's experience is not common among the bulk of Esperanza's students, though it is familiar to many of the school's highest achievers. As the stories in this book will show, many low-income first-generation college-goers have parents who support their educational endeavors but possess little understanding of what it takes for their children to get admitted to college. These parents, most of whom are immigrants, want nothing more than for their children to succeed academically and have a better quality of life, but many are unclear as to how to help make this happen. In a neighborhood where most residents work multiple jobs to make ends meet, survival is often their first priority.

THE SCHEDULE

Rrriiinnnggg!!! A loud bell signals that second period is over and Nutrition (a 20-minute snack break in the middle of the morning) is about to begin. Students pour into the hallways and out to the Senior Quad. When observing the students, there are some aspects of the school that are more evident than others. Many Esperanza students are involved in extracurricular activities, indicated by the cheerleading sweaters, football jerseys, and JROTC uniforms worn by many of the students. There are posters and flyers attached to walls outside advertising Esperanza's homecoming and upcoming variety show, demonstrating school spirit encouraged by both students and staff. One need not be a particularly keen observer to also note that this school is over-crowded with over 3,000 students present on any given school day.

What may be less evident are the various challenges that Esperanza's teachers, administrators, staff, and students face on a daily basis. All of the students here are from low-income families. Nearly 15% of the students at the school are from families that receive Aid to Families with Dependent Children (AFDC), while 80% of the student population qualifies for the free and reduced-price lunch program. As a result of their families' modest incomes, many Esperanza seniors describe having to choose between partici-pating in extracurricular activities or getting a job to pay for their senior year expenses such as prom, "Grad Night," and their senior trip. These are choices that students from more affluent backgrounds are unlikely to face.

Overcrowding is a major issue at Esperanza and has been for more than 20 years. The Los Angeles Unified School District deems a school "full" when at least 30% of its classrooms are in use during a given period. When overcrowding is at its worst, 93% of Esperanza's classrooms are in use each period. Because Esperanza's student population exceeds 5,000 students, it must operate on a multi-track schedule to prevent them all from being on campus at the same time. The multi-track schedule, adopted in 1982, enables the school to serve more students than the school has space for over the period of the calendar year. Multi-track (a.k.a. "year-round") schedules mean three or four tracks of students and teachers are staggered throughout the year with one track always rotating off for vacation. Esperanza's head coun-selor contends that the multi-track schedule leaves most students at a disad-vantage with regard to college and financial aid applications. Many simply are not present at the most crucial times of the application season. For example, students may miss application deadlines or fail to receive information because they are off-track. The college counselor explained that the B-track misses the college application process, the A-track misses the FAFSA application process, and C-track misses the college decision-making process.

The three-track schedule creates a multitude of other problems, including getting grades in on time so that students are placed properly the following semester, and forcing teachers and students to be uprooted to new classrooms every two months. Few teachers have classrooms of their own the entire year and some carry all of their materials from one room to another throughout the day due to space limitations. Another complication of the multi-track schedule is that not all courses are offered on all three tracks. This means that students must take classes during intersession, which would normally be their vacation time. In particular, students often "cross-tracks" to take AP courses during their vacation. Many honors and AP students at Esperanza High School discuss graduating without ever taking a vacation during their four years of high school.

Instability is a hallmark of the multi-track schedule, which tends to be implemented in schools where the students are most in need of stability. Originally built in 1923, Esperanza housed only 500 students when it first opened. Despite remodeling to add more buildings and classrooms, Esperanza remains the smallest school in the district in terms of land size (12–13 acres) yet it houses the largest number of students.

One might call Esperanza a 24/7 school because although the school-day lasts from 7:30 A.M. to 3:30 P.M., the school's buildings are also used after school, evenings, and on weekends for extracurricular activities and adult school courses. In fact, many Esperanza students and their families, siblings, and neighbors take ESL, GED, vocational, and remedial courses at the Esperanza Adult School. These classes operate on campus Monday through Friday from 8 A.M. to 9 P.M. and on Saturdays from 8 A.M. to 12:30 P.M. The adult school serves close to 20,000 students each year—1,500 of whom are Esperanza High School students. The wear and tear on the school's facilities as a result of its being used so extensively has clearly taken a toll over the years.

One Esperanza administrator expressed his frustration about the fact that proposals for school vouchers or private schools as alternatives to public education do nothing to address existing problems. Rather, they serve to perpetuate these problems by turning people's attention away from them. Similarly, parents' decisions to send their more academically inclined children to schools outside of their neighborhood affect the level of education that the school provides. For example, the Gifted Program at Esperanza has decreased in size over the last few years because many parents have chosen to send their children to schools in other areas. Incoming Esperanza students will consequently have less access to higher-level classes, which then has an effect on the course offerings for the following years. As fewer students are achieving at the level necessary to enroll in honors and advanced placement courses, these courses may begin to be seen as unnecessary.

THE STUDENTS

Student social support networks made up of teachers, counselors, and peers are the keys to academic success in an environment where survival of the fittest is often the reality. When asked, many of Esperanza's juniors and seniors claim to want to go to four-year universities. However, the fact that less than 50% of those who graduate will go on to college at all, and that 40% of Esperanza's college-goers go on to community college, are signs that few of them have any idea about what to do to get to a university. What is more, a close examination of many of these same students' cumulative records reveals that it is questionable whether they will graduate from high school, let alone be eligible for admission to a four-year college or university. They simply do not understand how the system works nor do they know to whom to go for answers to their questions. The average Esperanza student takes the courses their overburdened "track counselors" program them into, failing to question whether or not these courses will help them achieve their purported goals.

Esperanza's students rarely seek out or receive college-related information until their junior or senior year in high school. Typically the college counselor will make visits to junior and senior English classes to provide information about college requirements and financial aid. Consequently, if students get to their third or fourth year in high school having taken the necessary courses for eligibility to attend a four-year university, typically they have done so by being high achievers who were targeted to receive college information early on in high school by standing out academically. As a result, a college support network is more likely to be created for them by concerned adults and like-minded peers. The average Esperanza student will rarely receive this information until it is too late.

During the summer of 2004, twenty-two 9th graders from Esperanza High School attended a three-day college preparation seminar on our campus. Most of these students came because it was an opportunity to spend the weekend at a university and away from home. Few had ever thought that they would go to college due to poor past academic performance. What they learned during their visit was that college was still an option for them and they were provided the information and support necessary to begin viewing themselves as potential college-goers. While these students have become a small network who can support one another down the college path, they are only 22 students who make up less than 1% of Esperanza's 2,500 9ᵗʰ graders. Although a small number of Esperanza's non-AP students may apply to college, most are left to navigate the college preparation and applications processes on their own because few of them have family members who can provide them with any assistance.

THE SCHOOL PERSONNEL

When I first began visiting Esperanza, I scheduled interviews with five of the school's eight assistant principals. Among this group were two white men, one white woman, one Mexican woman, and one Cuban man. These individuals painted a picture of Esperanza as a school facing many challenges run by a very unified and cooperative group of teachers, administrators, and classified staff. I received a very different message from the teachers who describe Esperanza as extremely dysfunctional with factions of administrators and teachers, each with their own agenda. Indeed, many of Esperanza's 250 teachers, despite a genuine interest in the well-being of their students, are frustrated and disillusioned with the politics and educational bureaucracy that complicate their ability to do their jobs.

Esperanza High School is plagued by internal battles among teachers, counselors, and administrators. The administration reprimands teachers for the high dropout rates among students but does little to support them and in some instances may exacerbate existing tensions between groups of teachers. One veteran AP teacher contends that if the school were really invested in developing a top-notch AP program it would work to settle "turf wars" between the school's "Academy" and Advanced Placement programs which have led to teachers denying their students the privilege of participating in both.

The incessant turnover of track counselors—20 different individuals have filled 12 positions over the last three years—creates a variety of difficulties for students as well. At one point in Esperanza's history counselors came from the classroom, which meant that they had some experience with the student population they would be counseling, the school's curriculum, and the school environment. In recent years many of Esperanza's veteran counselors have retired and those who have been hired to fill their positions tend to come straight out of counseling or social work programs where they were trained to counsel individual students. However, the reality they face is that their primary job responsibility is to program students into their courses. As a result, many counselors are unfamiliar with the students in their caseload and often program the students incorrectly. Students and teachers tell stories of students being programmed into courses they have already taken or that are far above or below their academic abilities. Consequently, many students get to their junior or senior year without having taken the courses required for them to be college eligible. Upon graduation these students will often enter community college to make up requirements they missed out on in high school.

Teachers expressed their biggest frustrations about the constant state and district testing. Whether a small group, an entire grade, or a class are being tested, students miss out on instructional time, and teachers are held responsible for their students acquiring whatever material they might have missed. These complications cannot be blamed solely on Esperanza's administrators. They are charged with operating one of the largest high schools in the state of California in the largest school district in the nation; they are responsible for implementing mandates that come down from the state, the LAUSD, and a smaller mini-district. The LAUSD has been described by many who work within it as a "monster" that is nearly impossible to run in a manner that will allow it to equally serve all students or schools, despite the fact that the district has been reorganized into several mini-districts. Teachers report that a bigger issue, however, is the "pass the buck" manner of operating on the part of school and district leaders. One teacher explains that Esperanza's administrators tend to place blame on the mini-district for unpopular mandates, while the mini-district passes the buck to the LAUSD, who pass it to the state. As this teacher asserts, the ones who suffer most from the larger structural issues are the students.

When teachers at Esperanza look at their students' school work they feel a sense of helplessness due to the years of quality instruction they know their students have missed out on. Teachers discuss the educational disadvantages their students have experienced since beginning school and how they have resulted in students consistently making grammatical mistakes that would be unacceptable in a high-performing school or on the college level. With almost their entire student body made up of students who speak English as a second language, Esperanza and most of the surrounding elementary and middle schools in the area lack adequate numbers of credentialed bilingual teachers to ensure that their students successfully acquire the English language. Consequently, most ESL students are immersed into "mainstream" courses before they are prepared. At Esperanza in particular, teachers explain that students who need instruction in their native language are more likely to receive it in their English classes, but are unlikely to receive such instruction in other subjects such as science and history due to a lack of credentialed bilingual teachers in these subject areas. Indeed, there are 28 Esperanza teachers out of 250 who possess a bilingual teaching credential. Therefore

ESL students are "mainstreamed" and forced to sink or swim with few managing to keep their heads above water—a fact demonstrated by Esperanza's graduation rates.

At times veteran teachers at Esperanza describe feelings of powerlessness when they consider all of the academic challenges their students confront. Their years of experience have shown them that they may not be able to solve all of the students' problems, but taking that one student by the hand can make a difference. Most of Esperanza's long-time teachers explain that they have chosen to work in this community because they feel like it has been abandoned by much of the city. Students describe teachers who go out of their way to help while others put them down saying they will never graduate let alone go on to college. When questioned about why some teachers have a negative attitude toward students, one teacher asserted that these are the teachers who have given up on the students and should no longer be in the classroom.

THE SMALLER COMMUNITIES INSIDE ESPERANZA

To create an image of Esperanza High School as nothing more than an oversized school with oversized problems would be inaccurate. In fact, within the larger school there are smaller communities that provide important opportunities to the students who are fortunate enough to be a part of them. Among these smaller communities are several Academies, college preparation programs such as AVID and MESA, the advanced placement program, the Newcomer Center for recent immigrants, the JROTC, the Senior Cabinet, Student Government, and many others. These communities not only provide students with greater access to information and resources, but they also provide students with a network of mentors and peers who can serve as sources of support in a school where students can easily fall through the cracks. For students, being a member of these smaller communities also means that there is someone tracking their progress, checking that they take the right courses to graduate or be eligible for college, and holding students accountable for poor attendance or behavior.

THE REPUTATION

Esperanza High School's reputation among the general public tends to be unfavorable. It is one of the most overcrowded, underfunded, and low-performing schools in the district. One Esperanza junior discussed her awareness of the school's bad reputation for crime and overcrowding, and said that if the school had fewer students, it would not have these problems; at the very least, she would not have to stand up in one of her classes due to an insufficient number of desks. The school's size and inability to provide all of its students with high-quality instruction has meant that less than 50% of any 9th grade class over the past five years has graduated from Esperanza, and even fewer have gone on to college.

The school's negative image among outsiders also comes from the fact that Esperanza's students are the children of the working poor. Parents often hold two or three service or manufacturing jobs, and 55% have received less than a high school diploma. Consequently, parents are unable to provide their children with much guidance and support in their academics, let alone college-going. Students from nearby schools recount stories of shootings on or near the Esperanza campus by gang members who are rumored to dominate the school. Although the school certainly serves students who identify with one street gang or another, I have heard few accounts of them engaging in illegal activities on campus. Drugs are also rumored to be readily available to students at Esperanza, which has been confirmed by Esperanza students.

Adults at Esperanza agree that when their students enter the crowded halls of the three wings and multiple annexes and bungalows, many do so more to see their friends and engage in the social aspects of high school than to learn. Even so, there are those who come because someone has instilled the belief in them that education is the key to a better future. As I pass groups of students in the halls of this massive place, I constantly question each student's purpose. Particularly in a school where over 40% of the student population misses ten or more school days per year, the fact that these students have made the decision to show up makes one question, why? How would an average Esperanza High School student answer this question? How many have taken the time to answer this question for themselves? Judy, a gregarious 9th grader at Esperanza High School explains that students begin arriving at school as early as 6:30 A.M., and many stay late into the evening because they would rather be at school than at home. Indeed, many Esperanza students view the school as a "second home" because they spend most of their day there. The low graduation and college-going rates of the students here indicate that their choice to attend school may be influenced by a variety of non-academic factors.

THE FUTURE

Although the picture painted here of Esperanza may appear somewhat dismal, plans are in the works for a variety of improvements to both the school's facilities and organizational structure. In terms of facilities, the school is currently undergoing evaluation for modernization that will involve creating a new building with 20 classrooms as well as making improvements to Esperanza's current structures, including repairing lights, floors, and the general appearance of the school. However, the organizational changes appear to be much more exciting. Among them are creating and placing all students in smaller Esperanza communities. Esperanza's administrators have recognized what the school is doing well (i.e., providing smaller learning communities), and they are adopting this idea for the larger school population. The goal is for every student to be part of a small learning community—currently one-third of the student population is not. The biggest challenge to making this happen is getting teachers who are attached to their teaching styles and practices to buy in to the "all academy" structure. At the moment, many of them do not, and they continue to resist change, even though it is likely to benefit their students.

As part of its plan for "personalizing the school" Esperanza's administrators intend to take on leadership roles for each of the three tracks, which means one administrator will take on the responsibility for leading and coordinating each track, rather than the current structure where they are all responsible for overseeing aspects of all three tracks. Esperanza's administrators also intend to work with the Student Government to find ways to make school more engaging and get more students involved with extracurricular activities. Again, this is building on current knowledge that students who are involved with activities on campus are more likely to attend school on a daily basis. Part of this plan is also to take more opportunities to celebrate student successes. Currently, Esperanza students take various tests (e.g., AP exams, Golden State exams) and participate in a number of competitions (e.g., sports, drill teams, JROTC) and students ought to be recognized for their successes.

One of the challenges that remains despite the efforts of Esperanza's staff, faculty, administrators, and students includes a lack of a college-going culture on the campus. Much of this may be due to Esperanza's size and limited resources (i.e., one college counselor for 5,000+ students). However, Esperanza is not without its assets as well. Many speak highly of the school's AP teachers, and I have observed them providing high-quality instruction and informal college counseling to students. Furthermore, despite the college office's limited staff and resources, it actually provides a great deal of programming and support to Esperanza students. Esperanza's biggest challenge is to figure out how to make college-going an aspect of every Esperanza teacher's classroom instruction and every Esperanza student's plans for their future.

From my time spent at Esperanza High School with students, teachers, administrators, and other school staff members, I have seen the variety of resources available to students including committed college and career counselors, dedicated teachers, and multiple opportunities for academic and extracurricular involvement. Still, the question raised by many adults at the school is: Why don't more students take advantage of the opportunities available to them? Is it because they are not aware of the resources their school has to offer? Have the students and teachers given up on the idea that these students can succeed?

Students report that there are three primary reasons why more Esperanza students are not on the college track. First, many students lack networks of support at home and at school that would provide them vital college information and instill in them the confidence that college is a viable postsecondary option for them. Students explain that many of their classmates are intimidated by ever-increasing college requirements and may forgo applying to college because they misunderstand the weight of their class rank in college admissions decisions. Second, many Esperanza students deal with countless problems at home such as poverty, physical abuse, alcoholism, drug abuse, sick family members unable to pay for proper care, and homelessness. Although there are certainly those students with more stable home environments, they tend to be the minority. Finally, because many Esperanza students work to help their families make ends meet, they often begin making money while they are still in high school. Consequently, students may drop out of school or forgo college because they believe they will make more money by working full time. Esperanza's college-bound students contend that their working peers fail to realize that they will make more money and be of greater benefit to their families with a college education.

Still, Esperanza's college-bound students admit that even with the support of adults and peers at school, the road to college for the first-generation college-goer is fraught with challenges that could easily have kept them off the college track. These stories offer insights into the challenges faced by Esperanza students and others attending similar high schools. Their paths to college may serve to answer the questions raised in this chapter and provide both policy-makers and practitioners clues about how to improve college access at urban high schools.

6

· · · · · · · · · · · ·

Zoë Blumberg Corwin

The Paper Trail of Lily Salazar

· · ·

BAMBI AND CINDERELLA

"My mom was doing laundry and said she had a surprise for me," reminisces Lily, head tilted slightly so that her long, shiny bangs gently fall to the side of her face. "They were in a cardboard box, like they had just been shipped to the house. Bambi and Cinderella. I still have them. I couldn't read them, I was like three, but I remember looking at the pictures."

I ask why she thinks her mom, Graciela, bought the children's books. "To keep me entertained, I guess."

"Have you ever asked her about them?" I wonder.

"I think I asked her once, but she was distracted . . ."

Lily and I sit at our usual metal table in the lunch quad, away from bees that swarm around trash cans filled with food wrappers and empty soda bottles. We are sheltered from the sun by the shadow of one of the tall, concrete school buildings. Lily and her friends have been complaining to administrators about the bees for weeks, but the hives have yet to be found. Over the past few months, Lily and I have strolled down to this table during fourth period to talk about her life, her , and this research project. Often, as we begin talking, she removes various papers from her backpack: FAFSA forms, bus tickets, photographs, school assignments, and bulletins about financial aid scams.

One day I ask Lily how she would begin a book chapter about her life; she suggests those first pages that she loved to read. Colorful images of

Bambi and Cinderella. Books enthusiastically opened by an eager, pony-tailed child, the beginning of her paper trail to college.

8 X 10 GLOSSIES

The hub of the Salazar household is the living room, the place where the family eats, watches TV, uses the computer, talks on the phone, and relaxes. The focal point of the room is a series of six framed photographs. In four of them, young high school graduates (Lily's older sisters) smile at the camera from underneath mortar board hats. The two largest photographs are of a five-year-old and a two-year-old, Lily and her younger sister, Nidia. Until they graduate from high school, these photos will suffice. Lily's older brother and one other sister have been left off the wall because they have strained relationships with their mom.

Sometimes her older sisters tell her, "You're living in paradise with your mom." Lily agrees, "if my older sister would have done what Nidia did [referring to when her younger sister pierced her tongue]—my mom would have ripped it if off her tongue. She kicked my other sister out because she pierced her nose." When the older siblings were growing up, Graciela worked longer hours and had less patience than she does with Lily and Nidia. Lily thinks her mom feels guilty about this sometimes. They are also the first to grow up with their father living at home; the other siblings have two different fathers. This causes tension, Lily explains, "They say, 'don't screw up, your dad is there. But just because I have this so-called complete family doesn't mean I won't screw up. So it's kind of hard trying to prove them right. Yeah, this ideal daughter, I have both parents. It's a lot of pressure."

One Saturday morning as Graciela prepares pupusas, a Salvadoran specialty, she tells me, "No sé como mis hijas son tan inteligentes [I don't know how my daughters are so intelligent]." As she stands at the hot grill patting masa filled with beans and cheese into round cakes, she radiates pride when she envisions Lily graduating in the summer. Graciela has never doubted that her daughter will graduate from high school; going to college, however is a bigger concern. Despite the fact that three of Graciela's children have graduated from California State Universities, Graciela is still confused about many things related to attending university. She does all she can to make sure Lily does well in school, but neither she nor Lily's father, Oscar, feel equipped to help her apply to college.

In El Salvador, Oscar worked as an elementary school teacher. After fleeing the civil war and immigrating to the United States, he sporadically works as a cook or valet attendant. Lily's mother, the main breadwinner of the family, is a seamstress. Graciela works long hours, sometimes six days a week.

When Lily was filling out her UC application, she struggled with how to classify her parents' occupations: "Would I put them under 'craftsperson'?"

"Yeah. I joke with my parents that I'm going to a c.c. [community college] after high school. They know I'm kidding." Everyone in her family, her friends, and her teachers expect her to go to college. "It's a lot of pressure," she confides. When she is in the middle of the application process, Lily begins to consider community colleges more seriously. She worries that she won't be able to keep up with students from wealthier high schools who she knows will be better prepared. She doesn't know how she's going to cope living far away from home.

UC APPLICATION—ELECTRONIC PAGES

"It's not only my parents but my older sisters and the rest of my family, even friends . . . I was asking a lot of friends, 'Well, did you do the application?' And they are like, 'No, I just gave up.' But they told me, 'You better have!' And I'm like, 'Actually I did' and they're like, 'Good.'" The UC application is a major ordeal for Lily. Everyone expects her to turn it in and be accepted to a UC campus, but no one guides her through the steps or follows up to make sure she fills it in correctly. At school, her Senior Cabinet teachers (two teachers cover the senior leadership class due to a year-round track system) raise their eyebrows when I ask them about Lily's application. "She better turn it in, she's amazing," one responds without knowing the exact details of Lily's application process. In the end, she almost misses the deadline and submits it electronically in the middle of the night on the day it is due.

Despite having started the application online in September, it takes months for Lily to complete the online paperwork. With her application complete, Lily almost doesn't write her personal statement. She thinks her sisters are too busy to help her proofread, so she doesn't ask them for help. None of her teachers verify that she has been working on the application. When I check in with her two days before the application is due and learn that she has not started her personal statement, I offer to help. Multiple emails and late-night phone conversations later, she completes her three essays.

Lily is a strong writer and clear thinker. She was more than capable of doing the personal statement without my help, but needed someone to prod her along. She shares that two of her friends also had filled out the application but didn't end up writing their essays, so couldn't submit their applications.

"At four in the morning, the system was still crashing," Lily remembers, "and then I started crying and my mom heard me, and she woke up and she was just there calming me down." Essays written, Lily still needed to submit her application. Graciela provided late-night support as Lily fought with the online submission system. "My mom was like, 'It's ok, just keep trying, have faith,' because I can have very little patience for some things. So she was just like, 'Relax,' because she knew I just wanted to unplug [the computer] and throw it out the window."

I ask Lily if she thinks her parents understood the magnitude of what she has just accomplished. She replies, "Not until I was done, until I kept repeating to myself, 'I'm done. I'm done.' They were like, 'Was it that bad?' They were always so busy they never noticed when my sisters were doing it, so it was just like they felt like it was their first time with me."

MEAL TICKETS

A bright yellow and red sign advertising "Tommy's world famous burgers" attracts hungry clientele throughout the night just down the street from the Salazars' apartment. Fans on the way to Dodger stadium, business people on their homeward commute, and a never-ending stream of locals sit perched along a line of red stools. Headlights turn on and off as people pull up to the drive-in counters. Cooks in old-fashioned diner uniforms bustle back and forth between the main burger joint and a smaller corner shop.

Since Oscar found work as a valet attendant at a bank, mornings have been filled with "a little more commotion" than usual. "He's the type to be punctual, he has to be there at nine, he wants to leave the house at seven. We all have to run around getting ready," Lily jokingly complains. Tensions have eased a bit at home since Oscar has been working and Graciela is no longer the sole wage earner.

Each morning Graciela showers first, then Lily. "I'm up. I'm up," moans Nidia as Lily coaxes her out of bed. If she doesn't move quickly, she's likely to upset Oscar who is the last to shower. The family's one bedroom is "stuffed" with three beds, a television, a stereo, a closet, and a dresser. Below Lily's bed are stuffed animals and deflated mylar birthday balloons; above her headboard is her special drawer, where she keeps her "treasures" and clothes that don't fit into her closet. "My mom's closet," she laughs, "is the only place she's messy. She keeps cleaning it up every month—and it keeps getting messy." Whenever Lily gets to the point where she "can't take it any more" in the crowded bedroom, she goes and sleeps on the living room couch.

Always conscious of the weather forecast, Lily often changes outfits a few times in the morning. Even so, she is usually ready and accessorized before Nidia. The two often share outfits—pink embroidered slip-on shoes, camel-colored beanies as well as makeup, purses, backpacks, and CDs. They are each other's confidantes, they make each other laugh, and they cover for each other when problems arise with their parents. Lily, however, often pulls rank on Nidia, especially when the younger sister performs poorly in school. Lily checks in with Nidia's teachers, counsels her mom about what Nidia needs to do to improve her grades, and suggests to Nidia that she work harder.

When they are ready to go to school, the two head through a locked, wrought iron security gate that shields their apartment building from the street and down the stairs to the bus stop. Due to their low family income, the two sisters qualify for reduced meal tickets and eat at school. When she fills out her UC application, Lily gains insight into just how tight her family's budget is. She is amazed that her mom is able to support her family on a $14,000 a year income. She and her friends discussed their parents' incomes when they were preparing their UC applications:

> I was like, "What's your income?" It wasn't anything big because we know we are at the poverty line, so we actually joked about it. So we are just like, "How much is yours? . . . My income is this low." We were just like, "Wow." We were just thinking we were okay, imagine those that are really, really bad. It was surprising, it wasn't anything uncomfortable.

BULLETIN BOARDS, BINDERS, AND CUMULATIVE RECORDS

"It's because the teachers have to move around each semester," Lily whispers to me in response to my scanning the sparse walls of her advanced placement (AP) American government class. A few maps, a student poster, and a large red bulletin board with nothing except the red letters declaring "Advanced Placement Wall of Fame" frame the classroom. Lily, with one clean sheet of lined paper spread out in front of her (no binder in sight), whispers to a friend as Mr. Holmby prods the class along in a game of current events Q & A. At the opportune moment, she responds to a question: "Political coattails!" "Exactly," exclaims Mr. Holmby, "That's what I was looking for."

It turns out, that's how Mr. Holmby met Lily and invited her into his AP class—he looked for her. "Lily is something else," he explains. "I recruited her to be in this class. She's the type of student who could easily be overlooked with the turmoil of our track system" (a track system, which in Lily's words, "sucks"). Mr. Holmby explains how students like Lily often get assigned a schedule and just go along with it. "I noticed something in her. Silvia too . . . she's another one of my projects." He acknowledges another young girl with a pierced nose and an off-the-shoulder t-shirt. "I look for

these students. I go and look at their cumes [cumulative records], their attendance. I look at their SAT 9 scores. And I talk to them."

Mr. Holmby is Lily's favorite teacher. He is a middle-aged, balding Anglo
American who often sports a vest and shuffles around his class. When class
begins, he greets students at the door. Lily is rarely late to his 7:25 A.M. first-
period class and elected to enroll in another AP class, European history,
because he was the teacher. He is a touchstone for her—and many of his
other students—in the large school. He was there, snapping photos when
Lily was elected junior prom queen. He's the one she turns to with questions
about politics and college. Lily swears Mr. Holmby had tears in his eyes when
he told her she had been nominated for a social science achievement award.
He is also well aware of Lily's "economic hardships." Even so, there are many
things she does not discuss with Mr. Holmby. He doesn't know the specifics
about where Lily applied to college, nor has he read her personal statement.

As Mr. Holmby leads his 46 students through chapter five in their textbooks, he draws connections between early U.S. history and current events.
When he talks about the pressure for extra soldiers in Iraq, Lily raises her eye-
brow and mouths "draft." She is politically savvy. A few months ago, we were
having lunch at a local community market, and Lily was drawn to an article
posted on a vendor's stall that suggested ties between then gubernatorial candidate Arnold Schwarzenegger and Nazi Germany. She described in depth
why she disagreed with his platform and the implications his proposed plans
would have for her community. She has also been active in the effort to ren-
ovate her high school. For a number of years, plans for updating the high
school facilities have been underway. Lily and her parents, with Lily's urging,
have attended multiple community meetings about the school's fate.

During second period AP European history, Mr. Holmby continues to
personalize the lesson by creating stories about his 35 students in order to
illustrate various concepts. The kid sitting next to Lily is suddenly a million-
aire who chokes on a hot dog at the Southern California fast food icon,
Pink's, and dies—thereby opening up a conversation about estate taxes.
Another student abruptly decides to forgo a college education and becomes
an artist. "What would you say to your child in that situation?" prods Mr.
Holmby. "I'd smack her in the head," says a girl. The students giggle, quiet
each other with a gentle "shhhhh," then express a host of opinions on the
matter. Lily explains how helpful these anecdotes are because there are many
things in the textbooks that simply don't apply to her life.

Oscar appreciates Mr. Holmby's influence on his daughter. "Casi lloraba
[I was almost crying]," explains Oscar when he describes his midyear
exchange with Mr. Holmby. "Le habla una maravilla de ella [He was saying
such wonderful things about her]." During the brief time allotted for parent-

student conferences, Mr. Holmby had raved to Oscar about Lily first in broken Spanish and then in English after realizing Oscar could understand. "Más fácil decirme en inglés [it was easier to tell me in English]," shares Oscar. He would have liked to have heard more from Mr. Holmby and asked some questions about Lily's college plans, but there was a long line of parents waiting to talk to the teacher. "No había suficiente tiempo para explicar todo bien [there wasn't sufficient time to explain everything well]." They only had time to discuss the basics before other parents started complaining that he was taking up too much time.

HOMEROOM SCRIPT, CARDBOARD ACADEMIC PLANNER, AND HALL PASSES

Sandwiched in between first and second period is homeroom. As a voice over the loudspeaker drones in the background, the classroom is buzzing with activity. No students appear to be listening to the list of announcements outlining college recruiters' visits, changes in sports events, and upcoming dances. Several students read the sports section of the *L.A. Times*. One girl, Ziploc packed with a bright array of candy, drums up customers. A pod of kids pores over photographs of a party they attended last weekend. The teacher, propped up against his desk, chats with students. Lily is busy. She does not sit down for a second during the 20 minutes it takes for the school administrator to deliver his broadcast. She and her friend Lorena talk about softball practice and Lily's visit to the Long Beach aquarium where they are going to hold the prom. Lily relishes her position on the prom planning committee. She dashes over to a cabinet in the classroom and pulls out a candle with dried flowers embedded in the wax. "These could be the favors for prom, what do you think?" She asks Lorena.

Most homerooms proceed like this one. Students are supposed to listen to important information about schedule changes, extracurricular events, and college. None do. Still, some good does come out of the short period. Lily gets a head start on her Senior Cabinet duties and gets to catch up with friends. Every year, all students are given academic planners in homeroom. Lily has hers clipped into the front of her school binder. She shows me, "They give you the requirements to graduate, which is of course what everybody is worried about, and then from there in the next page it shows you the requirements for college," she says as she flips the thick, shiny paper over. "That's how I knew, otherwise I would've had no clue. Most people barely found out their senior year what the requirements were."

The large number of students at Esperanza directly affects the services provided to students. Despite the fact that Lily is in the academic top 10% of her high school, on one site visit, I ask Lily's assigned guidance counselor a question about her. "Lily Salazar, is she in special ed?" he responds. The counselor, who bemoans the fact that he spends much more time with problem cases than academically stable and college-bound students, is not someone Lily approaches for advice. On another day, Lily sits with a student who needs help on his California State University application. It is due the next day. As we walk away, she tells me, "You know, his counselor straight up told him, 'You aren't going to college.' He didn't take the right classes. He's not going to get in."

During homeroom Lily puts her connections to use. Because the one and only college counselor serves over 5,300 students, it's often hard to talk to him during lunch or nutrition. Lily makes a habit of getting hall passes out of homeroom or fourth period to check in with him. "It's really important to make sure he knows that you're serious about college," she clarifies. "You gotta be on his good side." Because she's on his radar screen, Mr. Bowman summons Lily out of class when recruiters come to campus and makes time to answer her questions. "He's the best—the coolest," Lily says as we walk by his office. "He tries to speak Spanish and keep students informed about lots of stuff." The problem is, Lily explains, that because of her schedule, she was off-track during college application season. So despite her comfort level with Mr. Bowman, he was often out of the office visiting classrooms at the times she was on campus. Similar time conflicts have also been the case with teachers who might have helped her on her personal statement for the UC application.

Later on in the year, Mr. Bowman is called to active duty to fight "The War on Terror." During the height of college rejection/acceptance season, when students are in dire need of fee waivers, information about specific colleges, and general support, their college counselor is miles away. "On Mr. Bowman's last day, I had to baby-sit, so I wasn't at school," Lily recalls one day when we are trying to figure out how to decipher her FAFSA award. "I called the office to say goodbye and he wasn't there—he was making his rounds with the other teachers. A few hours later his son called me back and they met me at Tommy's." Lily knows Mr. Bowman's 12-year-old son from when he spent time with his Dad on campus during vacations. The three talked about Lily's plans for next year and what the following year might hold in store for Mr. Bowman. "That would be the best surprise, if he made it to graduation. All the students would be so happy," she sighs.

FAFSA FORMS

When the time comes to submit her financial aid applications, Lily, as usual, makes the most of her school connections. She meets with aides in the counseling office to get the correct waivers and forms. She attends a financial aid workshop with her parents, arriving with most of her application filled out already. They sit in the second row, Graciela sandwiched between Oscar and her daughter. Graciela gets teary-eyed when the local Congresswoman addresses the packed school cafeteria and acknowledges the value of all the family members in the room. Unfortunately Lily needs more specific information about the forms than the workshop provides. Because Mr. Bowman had already left for his military service and she can't make phone calls during the day to the FAFSA office, she is left extremely confused about applying for financial aid. Bit by bit she pieces together information from various sources and submits her FAFSA and CalGrant applications. She goes online, asks her sister for advice and compares notes with friends. Luckily her efforts pay off months later when she is awarded enough grants and loans to cover her entire first year of college.

POETRY AND AP EXAMS

As Lily introduces me to Ms. Lareu, her AP English teacher, Ms. Lareu says, "A few people in this class will go to college. Lily is one of them, even if I have to get up and carry her every day." Last semester Lily just attended class and didn't participate in discussion. Now she frequently responds to the teacher's prompts. Overall, students are reserved. Even though they are poised to participate (one uses a dictionary calculator to decipher difficult words, others sit with highlighters in hand), the class is characterized by long, uncomfortable pauses. "I just want to know what you think . . . I'm not armed," coaxes Ms. Lareu to no avail.

When I ask Lily about her renewed interest in English she talks about how she loved reading *The Yellow Wallpaper* by Charlotte Perkins Gilman. This was her first introduction to a feminist text. It was also the first time in two years Ms. Lareu had included feminist authors in the curriculum. Lily explains that many students don't feel a connection to what they learn in class. She thinks this is why so many of her peers drop out. "Take history. Because if you were to take a survey, it would be the least liked subject," she suggests as an example. "Because they can't relate to it, it's history that affected them, but they feel they have nothing to do with it. One of the teachers wanted to have a Chicano studies class here at the school, which I thought was a good idea, but it didn't go through."

Another class that didn't go through was a workshop offered on Saturdays where Lily volunteered. "Ms. Flores was bringing in parents and explaining what classes the kids need to take in the 9th grade so that they would know the counselors, whom to talk to, just introducing people to the parents so that they would get involved." Lily doesn't believe that the school supports programs that aim to empower students and the community:

> I guess it was controversial—they don't want the parents to know about that stuff. They transferred the teacher to another school to a different job because she started doing that. They silenced her, that was so wrong. We were just trying to help the community out because there is a lot they don't know that is out there.

One of Lily's career goals after graduating from college is to return to her community and "help people take advantage of the opportunities that I could not." In the meantime, Lily attends neighborhood meetings about the school district's efforts to reform their high school, participated in M.E.Ch.A. (Movimiento Estudiantil Chicano de Aztlán), a club that seeks to empower students through learning about their cultural heritage, and encourages her friends to vote. "We're in that group where we don't think we make a difference. I don't think that way. I just gotta be heard and keep consistent with it."

As the class progresses, Ms. Lareu holds up a copy of the poem they have been working on. She points out to students that they might see a poem like this on their upcoming AP exam. Lily has decided to take the exam, despite the fact that she feels ill prepared (a sentiment that unfortunately plays out a few months later as a self-fulfilling prophecy when she is unsuccessful in passing the tests). She wonders why they haven't focused on essay writing in her class. When she thinks back on her past English teachers, she characterizes them as "all bad, all of them but one, and he retired." None of them worked with her on how to structure an essay or build her vocabulary. More generally, she feels unprepared for college. She tells me:

> Sometimes I feel like I'm not ready for it and that's why I was considering a community [college] and that's when my cousin came into play and she said, "You know, once you are there, you realize it's not that bad." She was like, "You just have to challenge yourself and keep telling yourself you can do it, even though you put yourself down." And she went to Dos Rios High which is just as bad as Esperanza High, even worse. She was like, "I know you are always worried about I can't compete with those other kids who are attending college," but she is like, "There are always tutors" and she was like, "And don't feel bad for being in a remedial English class because you are learning and that's what it's all about." She was like, "You will get there, you will catch up if you feel you're behind." I was like, "Yeah, I know you're right."

Ms. Lareu directs the class to the next page of their thick, literary textbook and asks them to interpret a new poem. Lily shares her book with

Chris, one of her closest friends. Chris is a big guy with a gentle demeanor, a football player. He lives with his father, a tailor, in a one-room apartment. Chris's mother left the family when he was three. They turn the page and scan the poem. The two friends have taken most of the same classes since junior high school. Now they rely on each other for motivation and to figure out details about college applications. Together they decided to apply to all the same schools and will hopefully attend the same college. They have an informal pact that they will figure things out together. When Chris goes to college, his dad plans on relocating to be close to him. "He's been my biggest support ever since elementary school. In college, I'm gonna need him the most," explains Chris. Lily is looking forward to being independent but at the same time is worried about "just how far away I'm going to get."

LETTER TO THE PRINCIPAL

One morning when I join Lily in her physics class, she leans over to me and says: "The colors in this room are so dull, it's hard to concentrate, makes you sleepy, you should take notes in each class." I wink in agreement. A few weeks earlier I had asked Lily to pretend we were going to write a letter to the principal offering a few complements and suggestions about the school. Among her top priority improvements: "Liven up the colors with paint and have some plants that are living still—because it is pretty sad now—nothing like it used to be [referring to pictures she has seen of the old, estate brick campus prior to when a fire burned it down]." Also on her list were more social activities like dances and gymnastics, more counselors for each track and more Academies because "there you are focusing on what you want to do, your interests." She complimented the principal on renovating the football field and lights.

Lily does not have any vacations from school. She takes her regular C-track classes but then continues with AP classes during her intersession break. Consequently, Lily and her friends who take AP classes, or her other friends who have to make up failed classes, go to school without a break during the entire year. When she gives me a tour of campus, we run across an AP history class being delivered around a long table in the low-lit foyer of the school auditorium. Students sit around a long, folding table balancing binders and textbooks on their knees. Because the class continues through intersession, the teacher's regular classroom is not available and the class has to improvise. Even though Lily says that the three-track schedule "messes everything up" she is resigned to staying in AP classes and attending school all year. In her personal statement for UC admission, Lily writes about her overcrowded school:

Knowing that at Esperanza High one in every three students actually graduates makes you want to quit. We face obstacles in an overpopulated school such as cramped hallways making it difficult to get to class, classrooms filled to the maximum causing you to either stand up or not focus, and having to meet deadlines with only one college counselor serving over five thousand students. Consequently, it is truly hard to take advantage of the opportunities available. I am one of those students who has persevered with help from loved ones.

SENIOR BALLOTS

Hard to Say Goodbye (Boyz II Men), *The World's Greatest* (R. Kelly), *In My Life* (the Beatles), *I Will Remember You* (Sarah McLachlan). Martin, the C-track Senior Cabinet president, writes down the nominated titles for senior song on the blackboard. The B-track president hovers in the background. The heart of prom planning goes on during Senior Cabinet, fourth period. Lily explains to me that a huge source of frustration in Senior Cabinet is dealing with the tension of having three tracks planning senior activities when not all of them are there at the same time. A group of students will make arrangements during their time on-track—and then the other track comes back and wants to change things. Martin calmly writes the suggestions down and then moves on to a list of side activities for the prom—caricatures and karaoke are definitely going to be there, air hockey is a maybe (too expensive and takes up too much room). A few days later, the seniors cast their ballots and choose "Hard to Say Goodbye" as their song.

Over the last few months, when I checked in with Lily to see how she was doing, our conversations inevitably began with an update on the prom. The A-trackers voted on blue as the main color, she wanted aquamarine. Her mom was going to make her dress, now someone else is designing it. Prom will cost each student $85. Lily estimates her hair will cost between $20 and $30 because her friend is doing it, nails $15. Her dress will be her biggest expense. During one of our conversations, I ask if everyone can afford to go to the prom. She explains that many of her friends have had to sacrifice extracurricular activities in order to earn money to cover senior activities:

> Well a lot of people are kind of sad. They are playing a sport and they have to quit. Like this one girl was the captain of the soccer team and the past few days she's been looking real tired. Her dad and mom don't make enough. And she has little siblings to take care of. And she had to quit soccer to get a job. That's what they do, they just get a job.

Lily is careful about how she budgets all the senior year expenses and sometimes receives help from her family. After learning that Lily still hadn't purchased her senior package, her sisters and brother pool their resources and give her $100 as a gift.

As Lily scurries around getting students' opinions on prom favors, I remember the first time she and I met. When I arrived at this same classroom, she was on the phone placing an order for 350 hamburgers to be delivered the following day for a senior class fund-raiser. The teacher respectfully deferred to her judgment about the order. Over the next year, I never quite knew what to expect when I gingerly peeked into the class. One day she is dressed like a kindergartener during senior spirit week, another time she has just come back from signing up teachers to be in the prom fashion show. I have accompanied her to various offices to pick up a lost softball jersey, collect a fee waiver for the SATs, or check in with a friend who had been out sick. Sometimes she meets me with gray rings under her eyes from crying the night before. Other times she speeds off from our interview to jump into a lunchtime merengue contest, or to pick up an ice-blended coffee drink snuck onto campus by a friend.

When I ask her parents if they think her extracurricular involvement is helpful, they tell me that they are very proud that she is the vice-president of Senior Cabinet. They recall being told by her teacher that Lily "participa en todo—organiza todo [participates in everything—organizes everything]" and add, laughing, that they wish she was so well organized at home.

LUNCHTIME WRAPPERS

When the lunch bell rings most students file into long, rapidly moving lines leading to the cafeteria. Lily usually uses her lunch ticket to buy a sandwich and orange juice. The tables where she and her friends hang out are located on the edge of the senior quad, separate from the rows of metal tables where most students eat. By the end of lunch, food wrappers blanket the concrete quad. Lily chats with football players, basketball players—the popular kids. Some of them she has known since elementary school. In the space between the two tables, Nidia and her boyfriend share a sandwich. "Yeah, it's pretty much a privilege that she gets to hang out there," Lily points out. "She's only a freshman."

"I keep bugging my sister about what she has to do, I made her look at the application," shares Lily when I ask about her influence on Nidia. When Nidia was an 8th grader, Lily made sure that she signed up to be in the Academy program so that she would have the "better teachers." When Nidia earns low grades, Lily lectures her. Twice now she has asked Mr. Bowman to call Nidia in and put some academic pressure on her. Both times he obliged.

Carmen, Lily and Nidia's older sister, is also involved in their lives. "It's not that she has to get all her answers and questions through a third party somewhere in school," Carmen explains. "She has somebody within her family that can give her answers, the guidance that she needs in order to complete her task, or even if it's just going through the same high school peer pressure and things of that sort." Carmen stresses to me that her older sister, Luz, was her most powerful influence in going to college because Graciela didn't fuss over her older children the same way she does with Lily and Nidia.

SECOND SEMESTER PROGRESS REPORT

One night I call Lily's house and she answers sobbing. Lily earned a B in physics and Graciela is angry. Through her tears, Lily expresses her frustration that her mother doesn't give her credit for maintaining As in almost all her other classes. "She didn't even ask to see my sister's grades," she complains, "and she has Ds!" Lily has had to miss several classes due to softball games; that is why she believes she is now earning a B in the class.

Report cards are sent home four times a semester. Results determine the mood of the Salazar household for days. A few weeks prior to the B in physics, Lily's report card, boasting five As and one B, was proudly posted on the refrigerator. Last year, however, was a different story. In the middle of her junior year, right when her grades needed to be the highest for university eligibility, Lily's grades slipped. Lily still vividly remembers when her dad found out:

> Because every time my report card comes, that is the only piece of mail they open that is mine and I forgot where I was at, but I came home and my dad was sitting on the couch, and he was just like with the report card in hand, and I was like, "Oh, he got it." He was like, "Explain," and he was just like, "Forget it, I don't want to hear it."

She had lost her focus, didn't realize how important her junior-year grades were, and had no one to stress to her that she needed to get back on-track. In her personal statement on the UC application, Lily addresses this tough time:

> Unfortunately in high school, you have your ups and downs. My big challenge happened during my junior year. That was the year my grades had to be their highest. I was taking care of so many responsibilities that my grades plummeted. My father lost his job and my long-term relationship ended too. Regret is the only word I think of when I recall my grades. Yet at the same time I feel a sense of accomplishment knowing that I have learned my lesson. I did not give up. No, I acknowledged my faults and recovered with the support of loved ones.

Now that she is a senior and has a better understanding of college requirements, she realizes how careless she had been. She also wishes one of her teachers or counselors would have advised her to seek help.

On the morning I spend with Lily's parents in late spring, they are still concerned about her junior-year grades. She has already received rejection letters from UC Riverside, UC Los Angeles, UC Santa Barbara, and UC Irvine. "Yo me sentía mal porque no la aceptaron donde ella quiere ir [I was feeling terrible that they didn't accept her where she wants to go]," shares Oscar, referring to UC Riverside. "Porque se lo merece, porque es una niña excelente—no es porque sea mi hija [because she deserves it, because she's an excellent girl—not just because she's my daughter]." She is still waiting to hear back from UC Santa Cruz.

Oscar believes that the "F" Lily received in chemistry during her junior year ruined her chances at getting into a UC school. Lily admits to not completing all of her assignments, but also believes she should have at least earned a D. When she received the grade, Oscar had marched down to the high school and disputed the grade with Lily's teacher. He was unsuccessful in convincing him to change it. Lily knows that with her SAT I score of 900, she really needed to maintain high grades and is still disappointed that she let things slip during her junior year. Her mother encourages her not to dwell on mistakes of the past, "She was like, I understand, I just hope you learned your lesson. She never throws it in my face, my dad still does, he brings it up a lot."

SOFTBALL SCORECARD

Last year Lily was a cheerleader. After being caught with her boyfriend instead of attending practice, her parents took her off the squad. This year Lily decides to try out for softball and makes the team. Softball practice begins on the outdoor volleyball courts. The three coaches watch as the 60 young women warm up by stretching and running around the asphalt courts backwards, ponytails bobbing up and down. The head coach leans over to me and nods, "You need a 2.0 to participate . . . unfortunately, not all girls make it, although I can't imagine why." Lily had prepped me for this meeting. She thinks the coach is an "OK" guy but disagrees with his intense focus on softball. The other day she had missed practice to volunteer at an election polling station. Her participation was sponsored by her Senior Cabinet teacher through a program designed to encourage high school seniors to vote. The coach did not consider this a worthy excuse and would not allow her to play in the game that afternoon. When she was about to protest, her eye caught the younger assistant coach signaling her to keep her mouth shut.

She did.

I learn more about the coach when Lily and I talk about stereotypes. "So going back to the Latina thing, you get stereotyped a lot. Like you are going to get pregnant young and then there is the pressure of not having a boyfriend, you try and you just have to be really careful and that's what you have to put up with," she explains. "Careful in what regards?" I probe. "That you won't go to the point of getting pregnant," she replies. "It happens a lot and the coaches were recently telling us they were going to act like our dads because one of the softball chicks got pregnant. They asked us why we always pick the ugly guys."

Another perceived stereotype: Lily is proud of the fact that she's in the top 10% of her class academically. Yet she can't recall the time a Latina student has been valedictorian. She draws a connection between this frustration and larger cultural stereotypes:

> Yeah, in school it's difficult because like today, [my classmates] were saying that the valedictorian is always Asian. And sometimes you just have to give up and you say, I'm just going to marry a guy with lots of money. I've heard that so many times and it's very, very sad. I was kind of put down that we can never be a valedictorian. And it's like wow, now another barrier you are trying to break. You are just considered the girlfriend or somebody who is just kissing ass to get a high grade.

TOP RAMEN LIDS AND HOMEWORK

After softball practice, Lily and Nidia sometimes hang out on campus for a while and talk to friends. "There are so many people that don't want to go home," says Lily. "You should see right after school. There are so many people here it's not funny. There are like couples downstairs and I ask them, 'Are you waiting for someone?' And they're like, 'No, we don't want to go home.'"

This is also one of the few times Lily is able to see her boyfriend, Chino. He finished high school last year and now spends his time between attending Los Angeles City College, working at Jon's supermarket, playing in his band, and hanging out with Lily. They watch basketball or football games on campus, and Chino goes to Lily's softball homegames. On the days they hang out at Chino's house, they watch cartoons and listen to music (Chino likes the Deftones, Metallica, and Pantera; Lily prefers the Cure, the Red Hot Chili Peppers, the Beatles, La Ley, and Classic Rock). On rare occasions, usually if Lily cuts class, they go to the movies. Until recently, Lily's parents didn't know about Chino. Now they allow him to visit and are slowly introducing him to the extended family. Chino is stoic about Lily going away to college, "I'm sad, but I'm not going to let it get me down. I know she's going to get something good out of this." He encouraged her to fill out the application but wonders what will happen if they end up in different cities. "I tell her, 'If you get sad, just smile and don't try and think that we're far away.'"

Lily and Nidia usually make it home by 6:30 P.M. Lily drops her backpack by the couch and Nidia turns on the TV. The two trade off speaking on the phone for the early part of the evening. Nidia usually monopolizes the phone, talking about boys, music, and problems with her parents. A few weeks ago, Nidia snuck out to get her tongue pierced against Lily's advice. Their father still doesn't know. Graciela found out when Nidia's tongue got infected, even though Lily had purchased mouthwash for Nidia to use to keep it clean. Graciela was furious and did not allow the girls out of the house for a month, not even to run errands. Nevertheless, Graciela spared them Oscar's wrath by keeping the tongue piercing a secret.

Lily knows that she has it easier at home than some of her friends. "Being a Latina," she explains,

> You have a bunch of responsibilities, like once they come home they have to cook and clean. Like this girl had an opportunity to be a part of a club or a sport and she really couldn't because she had to go home and take care of her brothers and sisters. And that's really hard because sometimes you don't even have a chance to do your homework. And they have so much potential, and it's sad. And they can barely make it.

For the most part, Lily feels like she is free from heavy household responsibilities but not always: "Like sometimes I feel like I'm my little sister's mom because my mom is working and my Dad is like, 'I can't take that role.' So it's really difficult."

Now that Oscar works until 8:00 P.M., and Graciela usually gets home around 7:00 P.M., the girls are in charge of dinner for themselves. Frequently they settle on Top Ramen. When Lily hears keys turning in their lock, she goes to the door and greets her mom with a hug. She knows from the hug returned (or not) what kind of mood her mom is in. If she has to work late, that usually means she will be mad. In those cases, Oscar tries to joke with her. Sometimes it works and she cheers up, other times the two fight. Lily just tries to "block it out" when they do and watches TV or talks on the phone. If she ever wants to talk in private, she resorts to the bathroom or talks really quietly in the kitchen so that Nidia can't eavesdrop.

Oscar and Graciela rarely allow the girls out in the evenings. They say that the girls' social lives are dependent on grades, but Lily believes being female plays a major role in whether they are allowed out:

Because I am female. They told me so, my dad even mentioned it, "Oh yeah, if you were a boy I would let you go out and da, da, da, but you're a girl." And I'm like, "What difference does it make if you're a girl? You can get pregnant if you're a girl and if you're a boy, you can get shot at." I'm like, between a rock and a hard place. I'm so screwed. I say I'm a project where I'm the first daughter where the dad actually stayed. So they're more strict on me than anything but at the same time they give me a little more freedom than my other sisters had.

On any given night, Lily has about one and a half hours of homework. Mr. Holmby always assigns reading and she likes to finish it so that she doesn't have to take the big book to class. The challenge most of the time is finding a quiet spot to study. "My sister is a big distraction, huge!" explains Lily. "She has the radio on, the TV on, and she is talking on the phone all at the same time." This was particularly tough when Lily was trying to finish her applications:

> For the Internet, that is another problem. The phone, I don't have a DSL line or anything, so that is why I think I would have finished my application a lot earlier, but since my mom was waiting for a call or my sister was bugging, that was a big thing. They don't get it. I told my mom and she is just like, that it's ok—to do [the application]. So then I would start on it, and then she would forget and she would be like, "I need the phone."

UNIVERSITY OF CALIFORNIA (THICK) ENVELOPE

When Lily's classmates begin receiving their letters of acceptance from various universities, Mr. Holmby's classroom becomes uncomfortable for her. Everyone expects Lily to be accepted to at least one UC, but for weeks all she has to show are rejection letters. She was accepted to a variety of Cal State universities and feels good about those options. But still, her friends and teachers ask her every day if she's heard anything new.

Then, on the very last day possible to hear a positive response from a UC school, Lily receives a thick envelope from UC Santa Cruz. She's in! She calls Chino to share the news. Bit by bit she tells her family. First Nidia, then Graciela and Oscar, then her older sisters. Graciela wants to know why she likes "this school that's so far away." Carmen, Lily's older sister who attended a California State University, cautions Lily about the huge financial commitment it will take to attend UC Santa Cruz. Lily wonders if Carmen might be jealous of her opportunity.

During the next few months, Lily anguishes over her decision about where to attend college. Chino takes her to see CSU Long Beach—she likes the campus. She and I drive down to CSU Fullerton. After our tour guide points out all the Starbucks stations but doesn't discuss dorms or academics in any depth, Lily leans over to me and says "I'm not feeling this place . . ." She recalls her previous trips to CSU Northridge with her sisters and can definitely see herself there. What she really wants to do, however, is visit Santa Cruz. But it doesn't seem like there's any way her parents can take off work and make the trip. Carmen won't take off time from work to take her up there. Lily is nervous about being so far away from home. She has heard the campus is really different from urban Los Angeles. She talks to her friends who attend college out of town and sends letters of intent to UC Santa Cruz, CSU Long Beach, and CSU Northridge.

ROAD-MAPS, CAMPUS MAPS

Three months after Lily receives her acceptance letter from UC Santa Cruz, Graciela manages to organize a trip up to visit the university. When I ask how the decision was made to take the trip, Lily smiles, "My mom's always been the type that plans stuff out—always. I just say it, or anyone says it, and then she says, 'Ok . . . this and this is going to happen.' So my mom made it happen." Aware of how important visiting Santa Cruz is to Lily, Graciela decides to miss one day of work. Oscar has just started his new job and is reluctant to ask for time off, so doesn't go.

At first they can't figure out how they are going to travel up to the campus. Lily asks Carmen to take them, but she complains too much about driving and missing work. Then her older sister, Luz, inquires, "Well, why didn't you ask me, dork?" Lily, not wanting to inconvenience Luz, is relieved:

> And I just thought because she was getting into her real estate thingy—and then my nephew is on the side. And I didn't want him to go along because it was going to be like a long ride. And she said, "Let's go, it will be fun—and afterwards we can go to San Francisco or something." And I was like, "Ok."

So after work on a Friday evening in June, the five (Nidia included) climb into Luz's minivan and drive until Luz decides they should pull over for the night. The next morning, they check out of their Salinas motel, grab breakfast, and head to the campus.

As they climb the hill to the university, Lily takes in the green trees, the long distances between buildings and can't believe how peaceful it is. She remembers:

> We didn't know what to expect and it was nice because it was the same feeling with the rest of my family. We just knew [UCSC] was up there far and heard it was cold. It was comfortable to be with them. I wasn't alone. My mom—she was just like, "Oh wow—it's so open—it doesn't even look like a school, you

know . . . it's so fresh and so clean." And then when she saw the deer it was like the cherry on top for her. She said, "I haven't seen them since I was in El Salvador." Nidia was like, "It's cool, man . . . just don't get lost." My sister was just like looking at me and she was like, "Good choice." So they were really supportive.

Approval of the campus aside, Graciela has a series of questions for their guide. She is concerned about the dorms, shocked that there are men's and women's restrooms on the same floor and wants to know about security—how tight is it? How does the bus system works? And just how lost is Lily going to get?

ONE GREYHOUND TICKET

The day after she returns from her trip, Lily receives a notice saying that she has just been assigned a slot in freshman orientation in three days' time. She decides to go because she still has many unanswered questions about school. Feeling slightly more secure since she has seen the campus once before, she boards a Greyhound two days later and arrives early the following morning at orientation. As she makes her way through orientation, her newfound confidence melts away:

> I felt really, really lonely—like the other students' parents were all there. It was that culture shock—it was the first time I saw the other students there—that were also going to be attending in the fall. And I was just like, it was scary. It was intimidating, it was really intimidating. Like their families were there—and they were going to come back at this and this hour. And I didn't have that because I wasn't staying at a hotel. And it sucked because I had all my stuff with me. Like my huge backpack with my blanket and everything in there. But it was heavy and I hated carrying it everywhere. Where was I going to leave it?

Lily is the only student there without a parent. She is self-conscious about lugging her belongings around but doesn't have a place to store them. This is also the first time she has been surrounded by white students. "I just felt so out of place," Lily confides, slightly shaking her head. After a while she met up with another Latina who "was really nice—but she knew a lot of people from her school and she lived around that area. So she knew what it was like. And I hadn't seen anybody from LA. Anyone. So I was like, 'Oh my god—I'm the only one here.'" When she tells people she came by herself, they are amazed. "It felt good in a way. Like, oh wow, I did come by myself. But then in a way, like if they were saying it like, 'Oh. That sucks. You came by yourself.' I didn't know which way to take it, so I took it as that way, like, 'Oh. That's messed up.'" After a day learning about required classes and registration, Lily is exhausted. "Once I got what I needed to get done, I was like, 'I just want to get out of here, I want to go back home.'"

The next time we meet after her trip, right before we are about to say good-bye, Lily quietly asks me, "Do you have any advice on being so far away from home?" I am caught off guard. Usually so self-assured, Lily is looking straight ahead, genuinely confused by her emotions. We talk about making the experience her own, of it being ok to miss home. I share how I plastered my freshman dorm room wall with photographs of family and friends when I went away to school. She decides that she is pretty lucky to know she will miss her family; some of her friends can't wait to leave home.

TWO GREYHOUND TICKETS

> So I was calling for hotel rooms and stuff. And everything was so expensive—like the cheapest was like $100 a night. And we're like, "No way, that's not going to happen." And with one of the ladies, it was like a bed and breakfast. She's like, "Oh, are you a student?" And I was like, "Yeah, I'm going to be attending in the fall." And she's like, "Are you going to stay here for one night? What's your budget?" And I was like, "About 60 bucks." And she was like, "Oh, I have a house up there and you can stay in the spare room."

Two weeks after the initial trips, Lily and Graciela board another Greyhound bus to return to Santa Cruz. This time they are headed to the EAOP orientation, a weeklong event designed for first-generation and underrepresented students. Each trip provides Lily with an opportunity to ease herself into the notion that she is going away to college. The third trip is much easier than the prior two because Lily doesn't have to worry about her nephew or carrying around a heavy backpack.

When they arrive in Santa Cruz, the hotel owner's husband meets Lily and Graciela at the bus station and takes them out to breakfast. Lily laughs about her mom's reaction, "And my mom was freaking out. My mom was like, 'How could you trust him? How could you just call him?' And I was like, 'Dude, we have nothing else. Let's just go with it, let's see what happens.'" After Graciela settles into her room, she and Lily walk down to the main inn and meet the owner. She is a short Colombian woman who chats in Spanish with a much relieved Graciela, grateful that she can finally converse with someone comfortably.

Until this day, Graciela had kept asking, "Why did you pick this school?" On this trip Lily finally feels like her mom might understand:

> "it was just little signs." And then I started to meet so many of people that went to Santa Cruz—and that was the only UC I got accepted to. It was like coincidence. And then these people that are so nice to us. I'm like, "Come on, mom."

It's almost as if God put that path and he's like bringing all these people towards the university. And she was like, "Ok, I see it now." So it was just like this big awakening for her. Like she saw what I saw.

When Lily and Graciela arrive at Lily's dorm room, her roommate is nothing like she had expected. "She was like this hippie, vegetarian, redhead. Ok?" Lily giggles as she recalls the first encounter:

> She was like total opposite from what I thought. And I was just like, "Whoa." And we just stood in front of each other and said, "Hi." "Hi." And our moms stood in front of each other and said, "Hi." And she was just getting her allergies and I get allergies too. And that's how we started talking. And she was from La Mar. I hadn't ever heard of that place. She was a total redhead. You know I've never spoken to a redhead before. She was really different. She was really nice, really cool.

Besides Lily's roommate, most of the other students attending EAOP orientation are students of color. Graciela quickly befriends a family from LA, and they make arrangements to visit their daughters together during the year. Lily and the daughter hit it off immediately:

> The daughter was really out there. She was from El Salvador too. So it was nice. It was a nice click. She was like, 'Man, I haven't seen any pupuserías here. What's going to happen? We're going to have to learn how to cook!' [laughing] And she's like, 'How are we going to survive here? 'Cuz she was like the only person I met who was from LA at that time. Later on I met other people from LA. She was like, "This is no city, man. Like what are we going to do? It's so clean! There's no buildings around here." And I said, "We'll be ok."

The students congregate with their orientation advisors and Lily loses no time in joining the icebreaker activities. Advisors tell students they can request a 'standing ovation' at any time. Upon request, they run over to a student and instead of clapping, lift the person up. Lily thinks to herself, "I'll try it" and shouts, "I want a standing ovation!" Several advisors run and pick her up. "Oh my god. So cool!" she remembers, "but then everybody was too shy to do it—so they moved on." Unfortunately Lily has to leave orientation early to make it back in time for graduation. She is surprised that the university didn't consider the schedules of students who attend year-round schools when planning the EAOP orientation and is disappointed that she can't stay longer. Regardless, she feels really good about her third trip.

CASH

As I begin to tally the trips up in my mind, I ask Lily, "All of the up and downs . . . how are you guys affording the extra costs?"

"In total it's 82 to 84 dollars a bus ticket. And then for the first trip my mom almost spent like $300 with my sister for food and things. Yeah, it's really expensive—I didn't think it was so much. You know what," Lily continues, "my mom is a total mystery. She is a total mystery when it comes to this, she just always has money, there's always enough. I don't know what we'd do without her. She just always has the money."

"Do you think over the years she has saved it?" I ask.

"I don't even know. I've asked her. She just smiles and doesn't say anything. And I'm just like '[gasp]—she's amazing.' I hope when I'm older I know how to finance my money that way. I mean, there's my sister's 15 [Quinceañera] right now. And somehow there's always enough. And I'm just like, 'How do you do it?' And she's like, 'Don't worry about it, in time you'll learn.' That's so cool. And then the whole time when my Dad wasn't working, she did it alone. And we were ok."

PROM TICKETS

"Prom is the night where everyone looks forward to it, especially the girls. We all want to look so unique. And they're just trying their hardest, and it never comes out how they want it. And that's what I heard from every girl." Lily relives her prom night, shrugging her shoulders and scowling subtly as she tells me about the dance. After weeks of preparation in Senior Cabinet, prom finally arrives. Lily isn't totally satisfied with her dress, but it looks pretty against the prom colors. Then her hairdresser creates an overly fancy updo. Lily is devastated. Luckily the woman that helps her with her makeup is able to soften the style. Back at the house, Nidia sits on the couch, smiling, as Graciela and Oscar take photographs at the house of Lily and Chino. As they go outside, Lily quickly notices Chino wasn't able to borrow his dad's sedan, and they head down to the aquarium in Chino's old car.

At the prom, Lily is slightly conflicted about wanting to be with her high school friends versus wanting to spend the evening with Chino. The aquarium looks great, but she and Chino disagree over her dancing with friends, and the night falls far below Lily's expectations. "While you're there at prom, you're like, 'Is this what I've been waiting for, for four years? This is it?' It's like, 'Wow, no big deal.' It's just such a waste of money."

SOCIAL STUDIES CERTIFICATE

Back in April, Lily received a note in homeroom informing her that she had been nominated for an academic award. She remembers her surprise and her friends' reactions, "I was like, 'What's this?' 'Cuz very few people got them. It was weird. And I just saw 'social studies,' and like everybody already knows in homeroom how Holmby is with me, and they're just like, 'Oh, do you know who gave it to you?'" Later that day she bumped into Mr. Holmby, "Do you know who nominated you?" He asked with a glint in his eye. She smiled right back: "Thanks!"

Tickets to the award banquet cost $25 per person. Lily is frustrated that they are so expensive, but Oscar is adamant that the family attend and buys four tickets. As they enter the school cafeteria, Lily spots Mr. Bowman. "How cool! He got a leave!" Lily greets him with, "Man, you lost a lot of weight!" He explains how tough his job is, how challenging it is to work with injured soldiers almost the same age as Lily, and how hot it is in Texas. He is about to relocate his family to be with him, but his daughter doesn't want to go. Mr. Bowman smiles when he hears that Lily will attend UC Santa Cruz in the fall and says, "Please, please don't smoke weed when you're up there." Lily, nods her head, laughing, and says, "OK." Mr. Bowman raises his eyebrow, "I know people up there . . ."

Everyone at Lily's table (Oscar, Graciela, and Nidia—and Chris's and Martin's families) cheers when Lily wins the social studies award. Mr. Holmby comes over to the table to take some pictures, raving to a proud Oscar and Graciela about their daughter. Unlike some of the other students who receive multiple awards, Lily hadn't taken predominately AP classes and participated in numerous college preparation programs. She hadn't surrounded herself solely with college-bound friends. As Mr. Holmby pointed out to me months before, she is the type of student who could have easily fallen through the cracks, but didn't.

Because of the way Lily is able to bridge both worlds, her friends call her "cute geek." She writes about this nickname in her personal statement on the UC application: "I can be loud and desire to be the center of attention during a lunch activity and at the same time worry to study for an important test for my AP class the next day." During high school, she would sometimes feel frustrated that she was in different classes from her friends, "It's kinda sucky because they will be talking about something they did and they'll tell me, 'Yea, you were in your advanced classes.'" But she also finds it "flattering" when her friends seek her help on homework or college stuff.

YEARBOOKS

The morning of June 29, Lily wakes up and decides she has nothing to wear for her graduation. She also decides that there has to be a way to sneak her two older sisters into the ceremony because her four allotted tickets only cover her parents, Nidia, and her 18-year-old niece. She gives me a call. "Do you think it would be ok if I told the teachers at the gate that there are six of you coming from USC instead of four? And then my sisters could come in with you?" I am not in the least bit surprised. One of the things I have most come to admire about Lily is her resourcefulness. I plan to meet her sisters, Carmen and Luz, outside the front of the school, just down the street from Rosa's food truck, at 6:00 P.M. Lily thanks me profusely and heads to the mall with her mom and Nidia.

When Lily comes home, her phone doesn't stop ringing. Juliet, Lily's best friend since third grade wants to know, "What are you going to wear?" This is a big day for Juliet too. She is one of Lily's friends who never considered attending college. Lily playfully quips back, "Just a simple black dress. Just leave me alone. I need to get ready." Juliet wants to know if they search students when they enter the stadium. She wants to sneak in a beach ball.

An hour later, José, Lily's oldest friend, swings by to pick her up. They arrive at the stadium, frustrated that they are running late. No one else appears to be early either. As the seniors straggle in, many tote yearbooks. Because they only received the books the day before, students add their improvised inserts to the real thing. As Lily struggles to figure out how to put on the collar under her graduation gown, she realizes that she forgot to give her yearbook to Nidia to hold during the ceremony and runs to try and find her.

GRADUATION SPEECH

Lily gracefully maneuvers the uneven grass on the football field in her high, black, strappy sandals, finds her seat in the front row and thinks, "This is surreal—I just can't believe this is it." Her friends start singing "It's over, it's over now." She spots her parents in the center section of the packed stadium almost immediately and then waves to her sisters and me where we stand in the teacher section. Other students around her aren't as lucky and "are freaking out" because they can't find their families. Carmen takes out a Snickers bar, shows it to Lily and mouths "I'm going to be here a long time . . ." Lily pretends to be mad.

Lily has been selected to introduce Senior Cabinet. An hour before she left her apartment, she was still translating her speech into Spanish. She put Oscar and Nidia to work:

> And then last minute, my dad was helping me translate my speech—like a couple of minutes before. I didn't have the speech before—I couldn't find the girl who I worked on it with and my dad wasn't doing anything. So Nidia was also almost ready too, so they worked on it together, and they asked me, "Is this

what you meant?" So it was a family effort. It was funny. There were like, "How do we say Senior Cabinet in Spanish?" We laughed.

When it is her turn to deliver the introduction, she is nervous:

I couldn't really lower the microphone and I didn't really want to speak really loud. And then right in front of me, my one friend was gesturing to her boobs. And my other friend was sticking out his tongue like he wanted to make out with me, and they were in the same view as my parents—and I wanted to look at them, but I couldn't.

She delivers the short speech with her usual poise and grace and even manages to smile at the school photographer while her co-presenter is talking.

DIPLOMA

Juliet's beach ball is confiscated by a teacher just as the valedictorian says something that makes Lily teary-eyed. The girl next to her gently nudges her, "Oh, don't get like that right now." Another friend, Lorena, leans over from the row behind and whispers, "Stop being a wimp!" Lily's is the first row to be called up to receive diplomas. As she climbs the podium, someone official snaps a photograph of the moment the principal hands her the diploma. She is sure the principal's back was towards the camera. After she takes her seat, she watches her classmates file by in front of her and can't believe how "it went by really fast. You couldn't hear all the names, I would've liked to have heard everyone's name."

Martin gives the signal for the students to turn their tassels. "1–2–3!" Lily gently moves the green strands of silk over to the right side and throws her mortar board up into the air. Just a little bit though, not wanting to lose it among the other whirling hats.

TISSUES

"Yeah, it wasn't like I wanted to cry—it's just like it came out. Everyone was hugging. They were like, 'Hey man, this is it.' And I'm like, 'No, no it's not.' And then I hugged José on stage—so many graduations: preschool, elementary, junior high. And then Juliet, we just held each other for a long time. She said, 'You better not stop being my friend, ever.'" Lily begins to reflect on her future and how different her plans are from those of her friends. While she is nervous about being surrounded by different people, she is also excited. She has already spoken with her new roommate, a surfer girl from

Oregon, and started figuring out what to pack. I ask Lily if she thinks graduation has a different meaning for her because she is going to college. This thought has resonated during graduation, but she has been thinking about it all year. She remembers how she felt after the ceremony, when everyone rushed toward the podium and started embracing:

> Like there's some people that didn't actually graduate and they're just like, "Yeah, this is it . . ." Maybe because I distanced myself a little bit senior year just because I was kinda preparing because I knew that was going to happen. It didn't really impact me. It was actually a happy thing. It wasn't a sad thing where everybody is like, "This is over." A lot of people were calling me and they're like "[summer] sucks, it sucks." And I was like, "Why?" And they're like, "Because it's so boring." And I'm like, "Well, I'm preparing for stuff" and they're like, "Yeah, but what am I going to do?"

MARIPOSA GREETING CARD

The rich aroma of Salvadorian food greets the Salazars as they enter El Rinconcito family-style restaurant. "There's always a warm feeling when you go in. There's light and music, your mouth is already watering when you walk in," says Lily. She sits next to her dad and 18-year-old niece. Lily is sad that not all of her relatives are present, but she explains, "I was just so busy going from Santa Cruz and all, I didn't have the time to call everyone so that they could show up. And I felt really bad about that."

As platters of "humongous" pupusas arrive, Graciela coaxes people into recording messages for Lily on her video camera. The older sisters protest, saying they have already talked to Lily but nevertheless share "congratulations" and "we knew you were going to do it." Lily reflects on her sisters' comments, "I guess it was kind of expected of me. So they were like, 'Yeah, it's no big deal, we knew you were going to do it.'"

Around the time the meat and vegetable-stuffed pastelitos arrive, Graciela, still busy recording, collides with a waitress carrying a hot bowl of soup. The waitress, most likely burned by the soup, assures Graciela not to worry, but Luz blames her: "Mom, you see. You're always trying to record." Lily stands up for her mom: "She was just trying to make something we could look back on, 'cuz we didn't have that when we were younger." Graciela temporarily turns off the camera but switches it back on within the hour.

Luckily the episode doesn't detract from dessert. Lily orders sweet empanadas. Her niece leans over, "You better share." Lily scoots her chair closer to the table and sits up straight. It's time to open gifts. Flowers from Nidia, college supplies from a friend. Carmen and Luz's gift comes last. Since they live together, they picked out the gift's theme together: mariposas [butterflies]. Wrapped in a butterfly gift bag, Lily finds a photo album with a butterfly on the cover. They even give her a card with a butterfly.

Weeks later Lily and I grab a soda one afternoon. She has a flirty, sophisticated new hair cut, layers feathered to just below her chin. She is wearing one of her meticulously put-together outfits, fully accessorized with matching purse. "What did you think of your sisters' gift?" I ask. "It was nice. It got to me. I think they were saying that I metamorphisized to like a butterfly, that I grew up," she replies. "They even told me, 'Yeah, you grew up now.'" She pauses and smiles. "I guess I really have."

7

···   ···   ···   ···

Kristan M. Venegas

Dreams, Disappointment, and Drive

TRINITY BORREGO'S PATH TO COLLEGE

···

NIGHTMARES

After a restless night of sleep, Trinity pulls herself out of bed. She has been having nightmares again. This time, she dreamt about her application to UCLA and being denied admission. She is nervous, even though she knows she is only dreaming. She tells her mom about the premonition; they take these things seriously. When Trinity finally has the courage to check her status online late that night, she finds that her nightmare is true. Trinity is denied admission to UCLA.

Trinity's dream school has been UCLA for many years, and she worked hard to gain admission. "I wasn't even wait listed!" she would tell me later. She can't eat or sleep after learning of her status. She calls her friend, Gigi, but can't tell her; the words "not admitted" are too hard to say out loud. The next day passes in a blur, and although she wants to double-check (could she have read the electronic message wrong?), she cannot bring herself to read the rejection letter again.

MEETING TRINITY BORREGO

When I first meet Trinity, she is sitting in front of a computer checking the movie times for *Matrix III*. She looks up from the screen and begins asking questions: "Do you like sci-fi? Did you have a hard time parking? I asked Ms.

Willis to get you a parking pass so it would be easier to come here. Do you drive?" I am supposed to be interviewing Trinity, but already she has come at me with a list of questions. With politeness, she double-checks my qualifications, inquires about my past degrees, and asks questions about the consent form she has signed. When she is satisfied with my answers, she leans back in her chair and asks me another question: "Why did you pick me for this project?" Before I can answer, though, she is talking again: "I think that it was good to pick me because I am active in school and I'm in the AP classes. Since I'm MESA club president and kind of active on campus I know a lot about this school, plus my brother Clark went here too."

Trinity is about 5 feet 3 inches tall. She has long straight black hair and medium brown skin. She wears no makeup and parts her hair down the middle. She is thin and wears loose-fitting clothes, usually a black zip-up sweatshirt, a navy blue t-shirt, and dark blue denim jeans. Black classic Chuck Taylor's converse court shoes complete her unofficial uniform. Many days, she wears an amber-colored plastic cross around her neck. Her large brown eyes darken as she contemplates new ideas. The most variable aspect of her wardrobe is buttons. A "MESA" button or a button with an ad for the latest science fiction-action movie might be pinned to her sweatshirt or her navy blue backpack.

NURSE DAD AND FBI MOM

Trinity's father, Emil, had been working in the United States for almost five years when he returned to the Philippines to attend the funeral of a relative. During his visit, he met Sabrina, the woman who would be Trinity's mother. Sabrina is a small woman with great energy and concern, two characteristics that were especially attractive to Emil. She had attended an all-girls' Catholic high school, and was working with the Philippines equivalent of the FBI when they met. Although Emil had to return to the United States and his job as a licensed vocational nurse in a convalescent hospital, he continued to keep in contact with Sabrina. He proposed to her shortly thereafter and soon returned to the Philippines so that they could marry. For two years, Emil and Sabrina lived apart. They focused on saving money. Their first goal was to bring Sabrina to the United States. The second goal was to save money for the children they hoped to have.

Sabrina came to the United States in the late 1980s. Although she was college educated and had worked in an administrative job in the Philippines, she couldn't find a similar job in the United States. Clark was born first, and Trinity followed one year later. When Clark turned two and Trinity was one year old, Sabrina attempted to get back into the job market, working at clerical jobs while taking classes to become a certified early elementary school provider. During the first months of Sabrina's return to school, Clark and Trinity went to the home of a local babysitter. The arrangement lasted only nine months. In the end, Emil and Sabrina decided that they would rather makes plans to be with their children all of the time than leave them with a sitter. The parents made arrangements so that Emil worked the night shift, and Sabrina crammed work and classes into daytime hours. When Sabrina completed her education and got a job at a local child care center, their work schedule stayed the same. These days, Sabrina still works the day shift and Emil works the night shift. They barely see each other, but there is always at least one parent available to the children 24 hours a day.

FILIPINO-TOWN

Trinity and her family live about two blocks from Esperanza High School and three miles from the center of downtown Los Angeles. She tells me: "I live in Filipino-town. Did you know that? It's where a lot of Filipino people come to live when they first come to LA. We didn't move here purposely, but the rent is better. It's kind of weird because there are not a lot of people who have been here a long time like us still living in this area. Usually they move on to other places out of the city. But my family is still here. We moved closer to school about six months ago because they jacked up the rent at our other apartment. It is convenient because now I can just walk to Esperanza without taking the bus."

She identifies herself as an inner city student who attends an inner city school: "My brother was at this meeting for an organization that he is joining and they asked, 'Why do schools in the inner city have low self-esteem?' And they used Esperanza as an example. But nobody has an answer. My brother asked me those questions and I am like, 'Maybe because we are poor.' Or maybe in this community, people don't have a very good prospect for anything, which is true, most of them are not going anywhere."

SNAPSHOT JUDGMENTS

During one of our meetings, I ask Trinity to take photographs of the things that inspire her to go to college. There are three pictures that show her neighborhood. The first is a picture of the store front of a liquor mart. The parking lot is also pictured in the frame; it is empty and dirty. As we look at the photograph, she describes her inspiration: "I took a picture of a liquor store because, like you know, because of the LA Riots we have a lot in our kind of neighborhoods. I think that is what people think when they think of where I live. They don't think about how people live here."

Another picture shows a first-floor apartment with a line of laundry hanging in the front yard. There are adult and child-sized clothes hanging on the line. "I took this one to show that families are important and stick together in the inner city. I saw the mom and dad and the kids. But I waited until they went inside before I took it, I didn't want them to think I was watching them or something. It's kind of like how not only do people live here, but we have lots of good things about us too."

The final picture shows a food kitchen. It is a picture of the side of the building—a plain white wall with a sign notes the entrance to the kitchen. "This picture shows that even in the inner city we still care about people and want to help them." People in her area, Trinity knows, are eager to help others and themselves.

MY BROTHER SAID

As Trinity and I spend time together, I notice the ways her family comes into our conversations. In particular, her brother Clark is an important influence. He is a freshman at UCLA, the university Trinity also hopes to attend. "I take his advice because I don't know, he is kind of like a role model" Trinity explains. "He had a higher GPA in high school. He ended up number 15 in the class rank and right now I am 40. I am kind of competitive with my brother but at the same time I am not because I am really close to him. Sometimes it is just my brother and I." Often, as we sit in front of Esperanza High School and talk, Trinity starts her sentences with: "My brother said":

> " . . . it was a waste of time to take career planning as a class. He said you can take your other requirements and stuff because you could take health and career planning at adult school during vacation and finish it in eight weeks."

> " . . . not to do the FAFSA on my own, go to a workshop and ask them to help you."

> " . . . to join this new club for Filipino empowerment . . .'"

FAMILY POLITICS

"My dad watches the news twice a day," Trinity tells me. "In the morning when he gets home and then right before dinner. Then my brother, when he gets home like around six-thirty, he would watch like thirty minutes of the local news and then world news. Then my brother and dad would argue. 'How can you support Bush?' My dad is old and he won't change his views. And there are some people that no matter how bad a person is they will still support him. And even my mom does not like Bush because he is taking money away from the people who need it. My mom says that sometimes the kids at her work are hungry because their parents don't have money to feed them breakfast."

UCLA: A FORMAL NOTIFICATION TO FRIENDS

When the alarm rings on Monday morning, Trinity ignores it. It is her first day back to school since she received notice of her denial at UCLA. She skips a shower and forces herself into her uniform of jeans and a hooded sweatshirt. As she slips into her black Converse shoes, she begins to feel the panic rising in her throat again. "What will her friends think? Will anyone else have gotten in?" She briefly considers what she will say to her friends about UCLA. Just as quickly, she decides not to hide the truth from her friends. She doesn't want to lie.

As the bell rings, Trinity slides into her seat. She has skipped the early morning "hello" at the AP lunch table, going straight to her first period class. She's worried that Gigi, who sits next to her in class, and whom she finally told on Sunday, might have told the rest of the AP crowd, but it doesn't seem as though anyone knows. Before she can turn to ask, Gigi leans over and whispers: "I didn't tell anyone about UCLA. That is your personal life." Temporary relief washes over Trinity.

Before the first period ends, though, at least two people ask. So she tells the truth. She doesn't want shame to turn her into a liar. She also keeps repeating to anyone who is listening, "I know you think that I am crying, but I am not. I am just so tired. There is so much work to do for my classes and I am so tired, but I have not been crying."

By the time she gets home, she is truly exhausted. Trinity opens the door to a quiet apartment. Her father is taking a last-minute nap before he leaves for his night job at the convalescent home. Trinity goes into the living room and sits in a chair next to him. Clark arrives a few minutes later, and he calls Trinity's name as he enters their apartment. "Hey, Trinity, I have an idea, I talked to some people at school; they said that you should write an appeal and ask the admission committee to look at your application again."

THE APPEAL

Trinity has no idea what an appeal involves, so she peppers her brother with questions: "What is an appeal? How can you make one? What does that mean?" Clark explains that she can send in a letter to ask for another review of her application; she can send in more recommendation letters and a personal statement discussing her reasons for her appeal. Clark walks over to the computer and turns it on. He waits for the system to boot itself, then clicks the icon that will connect them to the Internet. Trinity again asks questions: "When will I have to turn it in by? What should my letter look like? Who else can write letters for me?" Trinity spends the rest of the evening reading the Web site. She finds general information on UCLA appeals because she can't find any information about exactly what to put in her letter. Though she knows better, Trinity decides to blow off her homework again tonight. She'll catch up with calculus, government, and all of the other classes later on in the week. She's not sure about her daily calculus quiz, but she figures that she'll do her best. Trinity eats a bit of dinner, but she never takes a real break from the computer. She is almost sure that she will submit an appeal, but she wants to talk with her teachers about it. Clark promises to check in at UCLA and get more information. "The name and phone number of an admission counselor would be great," Trinity tells Clark. "I want to be able to call someone to ask them what to write." At about 1:00 A.M., she finally heads off to bed.

The next morning, she begins to approach teachers, contacts her UC representative, speaks to the college counselor—she does not waste any time but throws herself into the process. Trinity tells the story to anyone who will listen and asks for advice from as many people as possible. Her calculus teacher, a recent UCLA alumna, reminds her to "be sure to offer something that wasn't in your application, something special and unique about you that the committee doesn't know." With this information, she is inspired to move forward. She also repeats the words of her government teacher in her head: "You aren't the kind of person who will be satisfied until you have tried every option." Trinity uses those words to push forward. When she sees me in the Esperanza hallway between classes, she stops me and says that she needs to talk with me as soon as possible. She makes plans to call me that evening. Our hallway conversation is brief, but I can see that something is wrong. Trinity's face is ashen. Her eyes are sunken and her cheekbones are protruding. I wonder if she has been eating at all.

FURTHER CONSIDERATION

Trinity composes the letter she never expected to send:

March 31, 2004

UCLA Undergraduate Admissions
And Relations with Schools
BOX 951436–0091

To the UCLA Admission Appeals Committee:

The purpose of this letter is to request an additional review of my application for undergraduate admission to UCLA college of Letters and Science. I was over-come with disappointment upon receipt of your denial letter on March 12th. Because of this, I respectfully request further consideration of my application and offer the following new information: a more detailed explanation of my motivation and commitment to attend UCLA, an insight to my unique individ-uality, and an explanation of my success despite my educationally-disadvantaged background.

Attending a world-class university like UCLA has been a goal of mine for the last nine years when my journey towards academic improvement began. I chose UCLA because it offers many enriching challenges, research opportunities, and individuals in a unique learning and social environment I have grown to love and admire. During my third-grade year, I was misbehaving and not completing assignments in class. After writing my standards, I asked my third-grade teacher why her persistence continued, her response was, "You're the future of this com-munity." Prior to that conversation, doing my homework, succeeding in school or working for the future seemed futile because of the troubled inner-city com-munity I lived in. Nevertheless, her belief in what I could achieve inspired me to accomplish tasks I never thought possible. Since then, I have become a woman who strives to succeed despite obstacles in school, socioeconomic disadvantages, and living in an educationally apathetic community.

I attend an enormous high school where there is no social hierarchy of geeks, popular girls, jocks, and punk rockers as seen in other schools. Students go around from class to class unnoticed and with only a handful of friends. But within these high school walls strives a girl determined to attend UCLA, and that girl is me. Who am I? I am a novice guitarist, and a Bruin at heart. My pas-sion for watching sci-fi movies and shows stems from my zealous curiosity of infinite possibilities for the future and humanity's potential when coupled with intense research and cutting edge technology. This would explain my interest in science and history. Other than being a "trekkie," I am also a booklover. When I do have time, I read fictional novels (ranging from 500–600 pages) by authors such as Anne Rice, Dan Brown, and John Grisham in a single weekend purely for pleasure. I am not the typical teenager who only finds fun in hanging out with friends or watching a movie I equally enjoy tutoring other students, watch-ing Lord of the Rings for the millionth time and playing my guitar until there are calluses on my finger tips. Although I live in a community where prospects of a bright future are low, I have managed to enrich myself with knowledge through books, science, and music in hopes of realizing my goal of attending UCLA, With my strong interest in science, I would like to eventually pursue a career in either medicine, biology, or research.

Since sending my UC applications, I have continued to excel in all of my four AP classes and have achieved a GPA above a 3.5 for the A semester of my senior year. This is because I have not let peer pressure of "seniorities" affect my grades or attendance in any of my classes. Although temptations such as waking-up late, cutting class, or visiting my local mall are strong, I realized that they only bring temporary relief from academic pressures. I have continued to do exceptionally well for so long because I keep my dreams of becoming a successful professional close to my heart. As a result, I do not let "senioritis" or anything else deter me from doing well in school. In addition to academics, I am also deeply involved in MESA (Mathematics Engineering Science Achievement). As president of the club, MESA has prospered by winning ten competitions and raising over $1000 in club funds. With the club's ongoing success, MESA has become the largest and most financially secure club in school. Being determined to attend and graduate from college, I am also making every effort to acquire funds for my future tuition fees. Recently, I have entered in several scholarship writing competitions such as the Ayn Rand Foundation, Alliance of Asian Pacific Administrators, and the Rotary Club of L.A. (I am currently awaiting their results). As for the community, I have become a weekly tutor for my academy (Esperanza Academy of Performing Arts) where I tutor freshmen and sophomores who have received a Fail in their progress report in either biology or history.

In addition to my letter of appeal, I have sent an updated copy of my official transcripts, a letter from the principal confirming my graduation position as a 1st honor student, and five letters of recommendation. These letters detail my commitment to education, my various extracurricular activities, and my community.

Throughout my life, I have never given up in school, despite uncontrollable factors such as an unstable teaching faculty, budget cuts to much-needed SAT prep programs, and socio-economic problems. I have come out to fight and struggle to ensure a solid educational future my entire life, whether it is fighting to open a Spanish 3 class or maintaining a good understanding of course lecture material (despite having three replacement teachers in one semester). I have come out of this community as a determined individual who will endeavor to succeed, as long as there is a hint of hope, I have also grown to become more compassionate with others, and more motivated to succeed in all areas of life. Although I may not have appeared to be a Bruin at first glance, I assure you that I have the heart, character, determination, perseverance, strength, and individuality of a true Bruin. Thank you for your time and consideration.

ACADEMIC MATTERS

From our first meeting together, Trinity talks about Esperanza High School. Most of the time, she describes school policies and practices, offering the kind of critique that is rare in students of her age and experience. At our first interview, she talks about the "hypocrisy of the whole school and how things are run." She is an astute observer of her surroundings, and a vocal advocate for her education. She tells me: "I argue with teachers about certain things, about the school administration or the kids here or how things are run in the whole school." As she continues, she has Spanish class on her mind:

"In my junior year, I could not take Spanish III because they closed it down because only 12 kids want Honors/Spanish III. They can keep a class of ESL of like ten kids open for them, but they wouldn't open a class for 12 honors/ AP type students! I had Spanish in 9th grade, in 10th grade, and then junior year, where is my Spanish class? I don't have a Spanish class! Right now that is why I only have Spanish III. Our teacher is really nice, and she is like, 'You guys probably don't remember this because it was a year ago' so we have an extra review which kind of holds the class back from learning literature and poems. I found out that is what you are supposed to be learning in the 3rd year."

A TRIANGLE OF COLLEGE ACCEPTANCE

Mr. Holmby is Trinity's favorite teacher. Every year, on the first day of November—the beginning of the college application cycle—Mr. Holmby presents a schema of college admission to his class. Then, on the first day of March, right before college admission decisions come out, he presents it again.

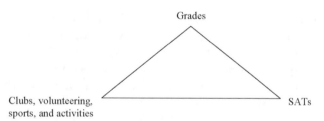

Sometimes the students accept it, and sometimes they do not. When Mr. Holmby reintroduces his triangle to his class in March, Trinity is still waiting to hear from UCLA. She uses the model as a way to personally evaluate her UCLA application. She believes that her grades were fine. She has a strong record of school service and volunteering. She is not as sure about her SATs. She scored about 1250. "Couldn't that be good enough?" she asks herself.

THE OTHER SIDE OF THE TRACKS

Trinity's school schedule is chaotic; it changes every six to eight weeks. Her classes begin at 7:21 A.M. and end at 3:30 P.M. During times when she isn't in class, she's in the library or in the MESA club classroom, catching up with homework, surfing the Internet, or doing something for the club.

Esperanza High is a school full of academies that run on year-round academic tracks. Trinity came to Esperanza as a "B-tracker." Even though she is on B-track, Trinity goes to school all year long to take as many advanced placement courses as possible. Technically, she is a B-tracker, but she takes classes in the A- and C-tracks as well. In the months of September through mid-November of her senior year, when other B-trackers were out of school, Trinity took three AP courses: government, psychology, and English. She also took two other college preparation courses: honors Spanish III and an art class called American images.

She also wanted to take AP calculus but she'll have to wait: "My AP calculus class is off-track because it is C-track so I have service for the next two months. I don't know why I am considered a 'B-tracker' because I have classes on all tracks—A-track, C-track, and then B-track. They ask me what track I am on. . . . I multi-track! When A- and C-track are on, I have government, psych, Spanish, and calculus. Our B-track classes, my AP English class, meets just twice a week. It sucks that my C-track class is during 6th period because I have to wait from 3rd period to 6th period for that class, so I just stay in school in the library and study. The sad thing is that I haven't had a vacation since 8th grade. I have never had a whole eight-week vacation since 8th grade."

In early January, the school tracks change. As part of her early spring schedule, AP psychology class goes "off-track," while her AP calculus class comes "on-track" for the next three months. To keep up with her AP psychology class, Trinity must attend special sessions after school a few times a week. Then, the tracks change again during the late spring and more shifts occur; all of her APs are supposed to be in session, but the schedule is difficult to navigate because two weeks are dominated by standardized testing. Because Trinity is a senior, she does not have to take the tests, but the shifts in time scheduling mean that she misses the regular teaching time allotted to each class so that in effect, she misses at least five calendar days of class time. This all occurs within a month of her AP exams. She is more than aware of the stress this causes on her academic achievement.

A WHOLE SCHOOL

The track system at Esperanza is confusing to an outsider, but for Trinity, it is more than simply a juggling act. Tracks are on her mind as she chooses colleges to apply to. "I am applying to six UCs, and then two Cal States, and then two privates," she tells me. "I am not applying to UC San Diego and Merced and Riverside."

"How come?" I ask.

She continues: "UC San Diego, from what I heard about it and what I researched about the college, it is a very unique college and the lifestyle and how the college is set up doesn't fit with what I want to go into because UC San Diego has, it is like a college within a college. There is John Muir College, Warren College, Roosevelt College, and each of those, it is sort of like academies, it emphasizes on liberal studies or engineering and science, stuff like that. I really don't want that because it kind of seems like I am going to another track school, you are kind of divided. I want to go to one whole school."

ACADEMY LIFE

Trinity is part of a special magnet program at her school. She describes the program: "'PAA' stands for Performing Arts Academy and they just emphasize arts like for example drama, singing, theater, tech, and dance and choreography. I am one of the closet-type members. I am just part of PAA but I don't do anything. I just take the required classes for PAA and college. The only reason why I chose PAA is because in middle school at the end of 8ᵗʰ grade, they are like, you have to choose an academy. I chose computer science academy, but that facility was not built either. . . . so then they made a computer technology because they had already bought all that equipment, but then they closed that down at the end of 9ᵗʰ grade. They said 'You have to pick another academy because we are closing this one too.' I chose PAA because I heard there is a dance class, so you don't have to take PE and they have AP teachers."

The same kind of problems permeated her junior year as well. "Yeah," she explains, "we kind of got screwed over. We had the Spanish thing that I told you about, and then my junior year, too, I had three chemistry teachers in one year. There was actually this guy from a local university—it was this 40-year-old guy who said, 'Hey, I want to be a teacher now.' Mr. Jamieson let him come in and teach our class for two months and then Mr. Jamieson became an assistant principal so another guys took over for two months, the last two months of class. I had three teachers, and we went over the same material three times. I could tell you anything you want about bonding and neutrons."

Trinity plans on a science-related major in college. After she receives a low score on a standardized test on the subject, she becomes even more concerned. When she completes her college applications at the end of November, she describes these events in her personal essay, using the magnet program fiascos and revolving teachers as issues of "poor leadership from the faculty." She uses these examples to show how "even though all this stuff happens around here, and kind of how this whole education here goes, I still did the best that I could. I talked about my personal maturing and stuff, and about growing some leadership skills too."

1ˢᵀ PERIOD: AP GOVERNMENT

After hearing so much about the challenges Trinity deals with at school, I wonder what her school day is actually like. As usual, before I can voice this interest, she tells me, "You really have to come to school with me and see what my day is like." The day begins in AP government, 7:21 A.M.

There are about 40 students in class, mostly girls, a combination of Asian and Latino students and two black students. Rows of fluorescent lights hum over their heads. The windows that run along the south wall of the room provide little light on the gray morning. The walls are painted yellow, and there are just enough desks for each student. When class starts, Mr. Holmby points to the notes on the board; he directs students to copy the chart he has created. Then, as students transcribe into their notebooks, he begins to take attendance—he doesn't call on everyone, he mainly says the names to himself as he checks them on the list. When he has accounted for each student, he walks around the room returning graded assignments.

The notes on the board look like this:

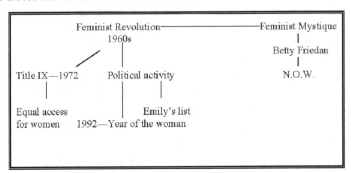

The students continue to write and talk about their grades and a new reality TV show. A boy wearing a leather studded bracelet says to Trinity: "Can you believe that she can't milk a cow? Well, neither can I, but I've at least seen it on TV!"

Mr. Holmby begins the lecture with a discussion of interest groups and group membership. "Why do people join?" He asks the group. He paces up and down the center aisle of the classroom as he speaks.

When Stephanie Pascal walks in late, there are no more desks available in the room. Stephanie has to sit in Mr. Holmby's chair. He continues to roam the room giving his lecture. Trying to encourage the students to participate in a discussion, he throws one-liners to the class:

On Special Interest groups: "The AARP fights for older people, who fights for you?"

On the California Master Plan: "Clark Kerr was a genius, he was anti-tuition."

On the women's movement: "Title IX is for every woman in this room."

On freeways: "Where the freeways are located tells you a lot about political power."

Trinity doesn't take notes, but she listens and participates. She will remember Mr. Holmby's words on the California Master plan a few months later when she begins the applications for financial aid. When the class is over, the students pack up and walk through a four-story maze of halls to homeroom.

HOMEROOM AND BANK TELLERS

"The whole school is supposed to read during homeroom now," Trinity explains. "But our homeroom doesn't care. I just take the newspaper and read. When I read, I overhear conversations and it is like, 'Do you have bank teller for 5ᵗʰ period? If not then you should check out of your other class so that you can take it with me.' I don't understand it, I am just like juggling classes here and they get to take bank teller, where they talk about banks. Bank of America comes in and teaches them. These students want to go to Cal State schools, but they don't even know the requirements, and no one is telling them. They are already seniors and it's too late and no one tells them. There was a meeting yesterday for the EAOP [Early Academic Outreach Program] but they didn't make it at a time when all of the seniors could go. I don't get it."

A VISIT TO THE COLLEGE COUNSELING OFFICE

Trinity and her friends don't really go to Mr. Bowman, the college counselor, for advice. She is still upset with him because he was at a football game on the afternoon that CSU/UC applications were due. Plus, he always refers her to talk to UC or CSU representatives rather than try to answer her questions.

When we visit Mr. Bowman's office together, there is a line of Asian students that flows out the door. The line ends at Mr. B's desk; he is busily typing in student ID numbers on his computer to verify students' grade point averages. The line moves quickly.

Mr. B says to the male student who is in front of Trinity in the line: "You have done quite well here," and he hands the student a set of stapled papers. Trinity is next. He turns to her and says: "I think that you would be eligible for this [scholarship], you should apply for it. Sorry I can't say more, but I don't have a lot of time today."

As we walk away from the office, Trinity begins to read the cover sheet. "It's a scholarship for Asian students. It's going to be so competitive. You know how it is for Asian students." But she decides to try and apply for it anyway.

BIOLOGY AND GOD

During one of our regular afternoon meetings, we talk about religion. She mentions that she is applying to Pepperdine University and wonders if that is a religious campus.

"Are you religious?" I ask.

"No," she tells me. "After I took two years of Bio straight I kind of turned into an agnostic. I am a Catholic. I am still a Catholic, but I am kind of open-minded and kind of scientific. I don't accept things unless there is some sort of reason to it. When I see some religion stuff, it is just kind of outrageous how people believe in that. At the same time I know why they would believe in it and stuff so I am kind of caught in between . . . My mom and dad are both Catholic. My mom did go to a Catholic school when she was in the Philippines. So yeah, my mom prays every day and yeah she believes in religion, but she is busy working so we don't go every week."

I look at the amber cross around Trinity's neck, and she explains: "When people see me wear a cross, I strike them as religious and I am like, I am kind of in between right now, kind of agnostic. I wear a cross because my brother gave it to me and it has some sort of sentimental value to it and not like I am religious. I have two cross necklaces that both have sentimental value; I am kind of close to my family."

I READ—DO YOU?

Trinity and I talk about balancing her weekends while working on her college applications and financial aid paperwork. She struggles to find time to relax and often turns to reading:

I read Anne Rice books; that is my favorite author. I read all of the *Lord of the Rings* books in 7ᵗʰ grade. I had this teacher, he didn't give any class work, any homework and all you have to do is read a book, at the end of the book write one essay about it. I was like, "This is stupid," and he was like, "Just read the book." I read the *Hobbit*, and I got through the *Hobbit*, and then I read *Lord of the Rings*—I read all three books. I was like, Wow! I finished three thousand pages! Ever since then I like reading, I read a couple of Stephen King books. I read *It, Something Midnight*, and *Tom Gordon*. From Anne Rice, I read the *Vampire Chronicles*. I am actually starting to read Oprah's books in her book club. I read *White Oleander*. I can't remember who wrote it. I think I want to read the new one in her book club, it's John Steinbeck's *East of Eden*. Do you read?

"Yes," I tell her. "I've read *East of Eden*. I thought it was good," I answer. "I like to read stories of people. I read biographies."

As usual in our conversations, Trinity forges ahead; she is always thinking, always asking. "Have you read the Hillary Clinton one?" She says. "That is one I kind of wanted to read when I saw it in the bookstore. That is also another thing that people tell me when they get into college. If you are a certain major, or you get higher up like if you are a senior or junior in college, that's your 3ʳᵈ year of college, right? You kind of have less and less time for a social life. It depends on what major you have. If I'm going to be pre-med, I won't have a life when I get into med school."

AP PSYCHOLOGY

The AP psych classroom is upstairs; it is a huge room, like a big loft apartment except that the main room is filled with long tables and chairs, a teacher's desk, a white dry erase board, and an overhead projector. There is a bathroom and sink, and a piano sits in the corner. Chalk and colored pencil drawings of flowers, fruit, and trees line the pale yellow walls.

Ms. Bordeaux stands behind her desk sorting through some student work; she greets students by name as they arrive. "I like this room," Trinity says, as she points things out to me. "What I really like in here right now are the lists." She points to two lists that are hanging near the windows that line one end of the room. "These are about gender differences, look at how much neater the girls' list is compared to the boys.' There is a gender difference right there." Trinity takes her seat and tells me that a lot of the students from her government class are also in this class.

Ms. Bordeaux makes a few organizational announcements and then begins her lecture. She talks about gender differences—the subject of the last class. She mentions "the fine art of male teasing" and says that it is very different from the ways that girls interact with each other. Then she moves into a discussion of Sigmund Freud. She shows a graphic to the class on the overhead projector:

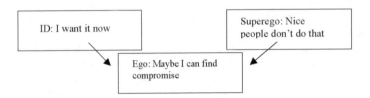

For Trinity, what happens in the rest of the lecture does not have much of a chance to sink in. She is exhausted, up late the night before completing homework. Sitting at her desk, she falls in and out of sleep for most of the rest of the period. She stirs when Ms. Bordeaux talks about Aesop's fables and "sour grapes versus sweet lemons." Trinity remembers these stories from elementary school and wonders aloud: "How many other people remember that story too?" Are Aesop's fables, she asks, "taught as part of classroom curriculum in Latin America or Southeast Asia?"

THE BENCHES OR THE TREES:
A SCHOOLYARD HIERARCHY

Trinity and I sit in the courtyard at the "AP table" during the nutrition break.

"Can you tell the difference in the students?" She asks as I take in the scene.

Two tables away from the "AP table" is a table full of boys all wearing basketball jerseys. There are a few girls at the table as well, also wearing sports inspired clothing. Next to them is a "couples table"—there are at least five couples sitting together. Right next to the "AP table" is a "MESA table" where many of the MESA club officers talk. Some of them greet Trinity as she passes by.

Then there are "the trees." From where I sit I can see three trees surrounded by students. There is a tree of "Goths"—students wearing all black, with dyed black hair and heavy black makeup; a tree of "Punks"—with multicolored hair, some with mohawks, wearing New York Dolls t-shirts and carrying Hello Kitty lunchboxes as purses; and a tree of "Rockers"—wearing Megadeath and Marilyn Manson t-shirts, most with long hair pulled into slick ponytails.

Trinity notices that I am looking around and says, "These are not all of the students. If you go downstairs there are more, and there is a whole other section for the immigrant students." I ask why they are not in this area and she tells me: "They stay near the Newcomers' Center, it's a good place for them to begin."

When the break ends and we walk to her locker to pick up her Spanish book, she reflects on how she fits into the social scene at school: "Me and my friends, we're not like the 'general population' of the school. We are the AP kids, the honors kids and the college-going kids. These are the kids like me, these are the ones who want to go to college like me."

HONORS SPANISH III

Ms. San Dimas teaches 3rd period Honors Spanish III to a class of ten students, eight girls and two boys. Two of the girls are Latina, the rest of the class is Asian. The Latina girls sit a few rows away from the rest of the group. Already fluent in Spanish, they chat during the first few minutes of class.

Unlike any other classroom we attend that morning, this classroom is neat. The mint green walls are unmarked and the classroom smells of Ms. San Dimas' flowery perfume. The desks are aligned in precise rows. The bulletin boards are sparse; only class schedules and language learning standards are displayed. The students in Honors Spanish III work toward these goals:

1. the ability to converse
2. the ability to write and read
3. the ability to prepare presentations and oral skits

While Ms. San Dimas notes attendance, a fire alarm goes off. The students stop talking and look at each other. No one moves to leave the room. A voice comes over the intercom:

Please disregard this alarm. I repeat please disregard this alarm.

"This happens all the time," Trinity tells me. "Students pull the alarm. It's stupid." Ms. San Dimas resumes, leading the class in a discussion of the homework. Most of the students say that they found the work to be "muy aburrido"—very boring.

A cell phone rings in the classroom, and students are tense. Though they are focused on trying to stay in the discussion, they struggle to find the right words. Finally, Ms. San Dimas instructs the students to open their books to a chapter on vocabulary about the beach. She asks each student to write a mini-dialogue with a partner about a visit to "la playa."

While the students work, the fire alarm sounds for a second time. Again, no one moves. Again the voice over the intercom: *Please disregard this alarm.*

Just after Trinity and her friend Anita present their mini-dialogue to the class, the fire alarm goes off for the third time. We all wait for it to finish. This time, there is no announcement. Students continue presenting their beach dialogues until just before the bell rings. Ms. San Dimas explains the homework due the next day as the students pack their bags. This is the first homework that Trinity has been assigned all day, AP classes included.

AMERICAN IMAGES

Trinity's 5th period is art, "American images," she tells me. The room is set up to be an art work space: Large cabinets used to store supplies fill an entire wall. Another wall is dedicated to artwork and is covered with pencil drawings of posters that advocate water conservation. "This is a mixed class," Trinity explains as students file into the room. "It's part of the main population of classes." There are students of all different types: freshman and seniors, students like Trinity who are doing quite well, and other students who are barely passing.

Before Ms. Fushige, the art teacher, gives any instructions for the day, Trinity has already decided what she will work on. She goes to her cabinet and pulls out her supplies. "This is an easy class. If I just think and get in my own head and not bother with what's going on around me, I can just work on my project and go from there. The teacher knows I'm serious so she doesn't really bother me that much about what I am doing. I know I'll get an A in this class."

Ms. Fushige asks the students to calm down no less than six times before the class is quiet enough to hear her. In order to get to this level of quiet, she has already thrown three students out of class. Trinity turns to me and says, "Wow, if you are taking down quotes, you'll have a lot to say about today. You will, won't you?"

THE APPEALS PROCESS

When she decides to appeal her denial at UCLA, Trinity receives full support from her teachers. One teacher tells her that "knowing her personality, she has to go through it, because she will always look back and wonder what could have happened. She'll never be satisfied."

Trinity is convinced that on some level her denial has to do with her low-quality school. She explains: "If we had better teachers who believed in us more, we would get pushed. If all the teachers were that way not just some of them, then we would all be pushed to a higher level, and I could have done better on my SATs. I know that if I would have done better on my SATs, I would have probably at least gotten in on probation or something." Trinity knows this because of her hours spent combing the UCLA Web site. She has written a formal letter of appeal and she knows she can include up to three letters of recommendation from her teachers, mentors, or others who know her well. She has also tried to a call the admissions office to speak to someone about the appeal process, but she keeps getting referred to the UCLA Web site. Thinking ahead as usual, Trinity has calculated that she has less than three weeks to complete her appeal and submit it no later than April 1st. In her estimation, this would give the appeals committee "one week to organize my file, two weeks to review it, one week to send me a new letter, and give me just enough time to submit my acceptance by the May 1st deadline." Trinity is very concerned about that national commitment deadline. She knows that all admission decisions need to be made by then.

The appeals process is consuming, often absorbing her for hours or days at a time. Sometimes she is concerned about how much time the appeal is taking from the other things in her life: "I am spending so much time on this right now that I can barely do my homework, and I don't really have time to try to apply for scholarships. There just isn't enough time right now. But I know that I have to try to keep all of these things going because I can't be weak in any areas right now, especially if I want the appeals committee to see how dedicated I am." In reality, the appeals committee will not keep tabs on Trinity as closely as she imagines.

GETTING LETTERS

As part of her appeal, Trinity seeks letters of support. She tells me about approaching her teachers: "In 4th period, I asked Ms. Dalquest to write a letter. 'Please,' I said, 'since you went to UCLA I know that your letter will be important for my appeal.'" Ms. Dalquest agrees, but she isn't sure when she'll have the time. The school is going to start the standardized testing schedule, and there won't be any regular class period for the next 12 days. Trinity realizes the problem of timing and feels another obstacle growing in front of her. At lunchtime she sits at the lunch table and tells a friend, "Ok, so now I know that my counselor can't write a letter because she's off for more than a month, and now Ms. Dalquest doesn't know when she can write me a letter because of testing. We waste so much time with testing. It's like two weeks when nothing will get done. This isn't just about my appeal. What about our APs? This sucks!"

Trinity vents her frustrations about her appeal, but she is also disturbed by the lack of class time. "How are we ever supposed to be prepared for college, to do good on our APs, and get the right classes and everything else, if we have to go to a school like this?" Trinity spends a lot of time working on her appeal, but there are other things that she needs to get done. She needs to get caught up in her classes and finish her application for financial aid.

SECOND CHOICES

The May 1ˢᵗ deadline for college decisions approaches, and Trinity still has not heard from UCLA regarding the status of her appeal.

Letters from other campuses have come in. UC Irvine has not accepted her either—another denial which truly baffles her. Trinity is in the top 5% of her class, surely Irvine would accept her. UC Santa Barbara, however, whole-heartedly accepts her into the class of 2008. "At least I got into a good UC, I mean, I consider that to be one of the better ones and it is close enough to home." Trinity is also accepted to a few CSUs, but does not consider attending them. "They were really just safety schools. I know that reputation matters, especially for graduate school. I need to start learning about that too, I guess."

Trinity accepts the offer from UC Santa Barbara, though she still hopes to hear a positive response from her UCLA appeal.

THERE'S SAFETY IN FLIP-FLOPS

A few weeks before her high school graduation, Trinity makes her first trip up to visit UC Santa Barbara; she attends an official preview day. "Everyone wears flip-flops!" We settle into a booth at McDonald's in the Mid-Wilshire area of downtown Los Angeles, and Trinity eats from a pile of super-sized fries. "At Santa Barbara," she tells me, "everyone is so casual; they don't wear regular shoes. Everyone wears flip-flops. It's so different. We don't do that here."

Trinity is surprised to see how people at her new school wear different kinds of clothing and how they symbolize different things. We talk about how it would not be smart to wear thong sandals; they are "weak" shoes. At Esperanza, you need to wear solid shoes to get around easily and also for protection for your feet. Trinity sees the students at her new school wearing these shoes as a symbolic shift, moving from her inner city high school onto a safer, more academic environment where people can be more free than at home. Although she still wishes that she was going to UCLA, she is at least somewhat open to these new possibilities:

"Things are different now between graduation and getting ready for college. At Esperanza, I knew how things worked, I knew what to do, but at Santa Barbara, it's really different. I don't know how to ride a bike? I don't know how to skateboard and those are basic things that everyone can do. I have so much to learn that's not even about school."

FINANCIALLY FORTUNATE?

Trinity sees herself as more fortunate than other students at Esperanza high school because her parents are willing—and most importantly, able—to help contribute to her education: "My parents will spend for stuff if it is education based. If you are like, 'Mom, give me a hundred dollars. I am going to go shopping at GAP to buy two shirts,' they wouldn't give it to me. If it is like 'I need to go to Staples, give me hundred dollars for supplies or whatever, they will give it to you.'"

In mid-November, Trinity received her first laptop: "My parents offered to buy me one junior year and I was like that is too far away from college, it would be kind of old, you know how computer technology is. So I was just like, I will just get it my senior year because there is like a $200 rebate, it was a back-to-school sale."

She also has an auntie who often serves as an educational benefactor: "My auntie gives me an allowance to help out for school and some fun. She doesn't have any children so she gives me and my brother money. Sometimes we get a $100 a month from her. I have used that money to buy SAT prep books and to pay for SATs and UC applications and stuff like that."

Although Trinity is eligible to receive free/reduced lunch tickets based on her family income, she does not meet the minimum requirements for fee waivers based on the College Board criteria—the testing agency for SAT and AP exams—or for the University of California or California State University systems. "We are less than $2,000 over the limit for testing and UC applications; I guess that means that we are low income but not low income enough." She ends up paying all of the application and exam fees. The yearly income for her family of four is less than $35,000.

FORMS, FORMS, FORMS

During the winter months, Trinity works on her financial aid forms. First, she completes forms for state aid. This is her first personal experience with applying for financial aid, and she is quickly confused and concerned. A college office representative came to her homeroom and passed out grade point verification forms for students to complete to apply for state merit aid. The representative told the students that if they filled out the top part of the form, that the college office would complete the second part of the form and then help with mailing the form out. But Trinity did not trust this process. "I am not going to wait for the college office anymore to tell me how to do it, so I did it on my own. I read the paper and tracked down the counselors to sign it."

She also plans to attend the "Cash for College" workshop, a local meeting scheduled for students and parents on a Saturday morning. She and her mom attend; they hope the workshop will enable them to complete most, if not all of the Free Application for Federal Student Aid form.

FREE CASH FOR COLLEGE: A DIGITAL DIVIDE

The "Free Cash for College" session—a program sponsored by the Los Angeles Mayor's office—begins early on a Saturday morning in January. Trinity and her mother arrive early and find a large group already gathered in the cafeteria for the opening session. By the time the session starts, it is standing room only. They sit quietly through the opening session, which is delivered in English and Spanish. Sabrina Borrego's most comfortable language, however, is Tagalog, and it is not easy for her to follow the conversation.

When the opening session is over, they head down the hall to the library for the "English only" financial aid session. Trinity walks a few steps in front of her mother, straining not to show too much impatience with her mother's slower pace. As they enter the room, there are two white women greeting families and students at the door: "Please hurry and be seated, you'll have to find a spot, we don't have time to waste." This is their welcome to the students and parents who enter the room. "You are already running late since that last session took too long." One of the women "sing songs" her words to the group as if they were a gathering of young children.

Trinity and her mother take seats at the front of the room as the representative begins her speech. She uses a timed slide presentation so that a new slide appears on screen every few moments. She encourages the students to complete their financial aid forms online. Trinity's mom raises her hand. "Is this a mandatory rule?" She asks. "How does it help the student?" The speaker laughs and responds: "Now's the time parents! Now's the time to finally get online and get that e-mail address and really help your students!" Trinity's mom sinks into her chair, drops her head a little and looks over at Trinity. Sabrina is embarrassed, but she makes a note to herself to be sure that Trinity completes her form online, no matter what.

A few days later, Trinity is still upset about what happened at the workshop. "I think it was really helpful, but I think they were kind of mean because of what they said to my mom. She is always smiling and says that nothing really bothers her. I don't think that white lady understood the inner city, and I think that's why she made that joke. Because if she understood the people here, she would know that most parents don't know how to use the computer, I don't think she would have said that."

UCLA RESPONDS

Trinity receives a letter from UCLA shortly before graduation. "Well, I didn't get in." She begins to read me parts of the letter: "After a careful review of your application . . . we have decided to retain our initial decision regarding your admission application . . ." The letter goes on to discuss the incoming class size in relation to budget cuts that are taking place in higher education in California.

"It's not very personal," Trinity tells me. "I wonder how much time they really spent looking at it? It's another big school, just like Esperanza. It's happening again, not enough money for a good school. I went to school at the wrong time!"

Her denial letter does note that she can consider applying for transfer admission after taking a few courses at a community college. Trinity wonders if she should consider this option.

IN THE MEDALS: GRADUATION 2004

My cell phone rings a few days before graduation; Trinity's voice comes on the line, and she starts asking questions: "Did you wear a lot of medals when you graduated? Do you have to wear them? Is it a rule? I have three medals and sash that I could wear. One medal is for California State Federation (CSF), another is for being in MESA, and then there is a general Esperanza one too. Plus I have a sash for being in S.P.A.C.E. Oh and I forgot, I have a gold cord for CSF too. So, that's a lot of stuff to wear. Am I supposed to wear it all?" Trinity is ready to graduate, ready to move on; in her mind, high school is already over even before the ceremonial ending:

"Once my last final is over, it's just follow the school rules for a few more hours and then that's it. My brother kept reminding me to make sure that all my school fees are paid so that I can graduate. There is a girl in my class who isn't going to get to graduate because she can't find her English book. One book that costs like $40 is keeping her from walking across that stage. You have to be really careful with the rules. And oh yeah, I almost forgot, they put me in the front, me and some of my friends. If you are in the top 20 or in CSF or something, they put you in the front. So if you are there, you can see me in the front. My dad is coming too. He took time off of work. My dad and my mom and my brother and my auntie will be there. So it'll be good, but I think I'm ready for it to happen now. But I have to figure out about the medals. Are you still going to be there?"

I am there to see her, sitting in the front row, fifth person from center. She chooses to wear some, but not all of her medals and sashes. Her long hair hangs straight and moves slightly in the breeze, getting tangled into the green tassel hanging from her mortar board. She wears a skirt under her green graduation gown and even shoes with a bit of a heel. She looks happy and relaxed. She does not yell and talk as much as the other students sitting around her, but she jokes with her friends and frequently waves to me and her family in the stands. Trinity tells me later that she felt "satisfied. Like I have accomplished something for the day, for that time in my life."

TACOS AND WHITE RICE AT UC SANTA BARBARA

Two days after Trinity has moved onto campus in Santa Barbara, she calls.

"Hi Kristan, guess what? I can't wait to transfer! Can you help me?" Trinity laughs while she says this, but the truth is that she really has not enjoyed her first few days on campus. However, she is still driven; she still gets things done. She visits the financial aid office. She attends a workshop for minority students. She decides to drop a class after reviewing the syllabus (chemistry); she wants to be sure that she can keep up her grades. She buys the books for her classes—$380.00 at the time we talked. Her aunt has paid for them. "It is so different here," she explains. "The food is bad. The Mexican food is so Americanized. I need a taco!" She tells me that the Asian food is not much better. "I am pretty sure that I don't belong here."

Already she is asking questions about the next steps, about how she might still go to UCLA: "Can you help me with the transfer process again? Like will you listen while I go through this? I saved the UCLA rep.'s phone number from when he was at Esperanza last year. I'm going to call him."

8

• • • • • • • • • • • •

William G. Tierney

Conclusion

CULTURAL BIOGRAPHIES AND POLICY-MAKING

• • •

We began the interviews and observations that account for the bulk of this text in the midst of yet another quite rancorous debate about the best way to ascertain the problems that exist in education and how to solve them (Shavelson & Towne, 2002; Mosteller & Boruch, 2002; Lincoln & Cannella, 2004). Although we do not wish to enter into that debate here, we cannot avoid it. There are those who will assume that we have done little more than tell stories, and that, while stories might be nice, they are irrelevant to the policy process (Cook & Payne, 2002). Even those who are sympathetic with the ability of qualitative research to influence the policy process generally focus more on intensive and multiple case studies rather than oral histories, life stories, or cultural biographies (Yin, 1984; Rist, 2000).

We also recognize, of course, the limitations of qualitative research in general, and cultural biographies in particular with regard to generalizations that might be recommended for all educational settings. At the same time, we are deeply troubled with an ideological stance that assumes randomized trials are the "gold standard for what works" (Whitehurst, 2003, p. 8) to such a degree that they are the "only sure method for determining the effectiveness of education programs and practices" (Whitehurst, 2003, p. 6). We leave it to others (Maxwell, 2004; Howe, 2004) to quarrel with the efficacy and plausibility of randomized trials; we also believe it is naïve to claim that those who have advocated for qualitative research in education "are probably a major cause of the impoverished current state of knowledge" (Cook & Payne, 2002, p. 151). Our assumption has been that behind, or rather in front of, these randomized trials are the faces of students such as Juan and

Trinity. The challenges that Jenny, Lily, and Mushutu encounter give depth to decontextualized analyses that may capture a particular moment in time but miss the dynamic environments in which these students are embedded as well as the complexity of their lives. Some may also suggest that a cultural biography is an odd choice of method to study teenagers. They are so young. How is it possible to develop a biography from the life of an adolescent?

I trust that we have demonstrated that the lives of these young people are intricate, bewildering, and complicated. Simply because they have not lived for many years does not mean their lives are void of familial complexity or that their friendships are simplistic or linear. The strength of Jenny's family surely was a factor in her applying to college; Lily's sisters, however, were at times supportive and other times noticeably absent in helping her navigate the route to college. Juan's father played a negative role in his son's life, but his father also imbued in Juan a sense of responsibility that held him in good stead in an otherwise chaotic environment. Mushutu's almost Messianic zeal for gaining an education seemed to come out of nowhere and at first was confusing to us, just as Trinity's reticence at reaching out to her friends for advice and support was a paradox. Adolescence, though, is a time of self-definition, and how individuals come to define themselves is no easy process that follows a checklist of actions complete with dos and don'ts.

Indeed, our purpose here has been to show the complexity of adolescent lives and to embed these lives in a social ecology of the neighborhood to highlight how fraught with peril the path to college really is. We do not deny that students from affluent families and communities have similarly complex lives, albeit with distinctly different dramas. However, at a time when virtually everyone agrees that the twenty-first century workforce needs to be better educated and that some form of postsecondary education is going to be needed for the vast majority of the citizenry, youths such as Trinity, Lily, and the others face a particularly perilous path. Their lives are unique and complex, but there are also intersecting themes that cut across these lives. These cross-cutting themes give meaning to additional research we have done over the last decade and suggest five broad ideas that warrant elaboration.

THE IMPORTANCE OF NETWORKS

First-generation students in low-income schools have fewer college-oriented networks and relationships to call upon than their peers who either have family members who have gone to college or attend schools with more comprehensive college counseling services. Going to college is not a singular event or moment that someone decides during the senior year. These five students illustrate that routes to college readiness vary tremendously. Mushutu became focused on college as soon as he started high school, and his teachers placed him in rigorous classes; Juan sat in an AP class not because he was a gifted student but by happenstance; Jenny navigated her courses relatively on her own with occasional input from her peers; Trinity took classes not because of any special trajectory that her parents or counselor placed her on, but because of decisions she made on her own about what she needed to take to get to college; Lily was recruited into her AP classes because of the diligence of a caring teacher; otherwise she most likely would have slipped through the cracks.

The challenge for these students was to find, or more likely create, a web of social and academic networks that helped them plan for college. Juan was the least networked; he wandered through his high school years without familial, academic, or peer support. The result was that he had no one to turn to when he found himself trapped by an unsympathetic legal system and an uncaring educational bureaucracy. Trinity had a series of weak networks; she seemed to drift in and out of them, and, possibly as a result of that drifting, received little logistical or emotional support. Jenny used school clubs and sports as networks, and her family as a support. However, when we compare the lives of these students with the lives of students in more affluent schools, the experiences of Trinity and the others pale in comparison. More affluent schools gear the secondary experience toward college-going from before the first day of freshman year. Students walk into the ninth grade with preexisting networks waiting for them; indeed, the networks in upper-income schools are not passive—networks do not simply exist for students to choose to enter. Parents, teachers, and counselors place students into existing networks because they will help their charges get into the college of their choice. These students would have a hard time avoiding being networked; class trips take students to colleges for tours and introductions, and groups outside of school help students prepare to write college essays or undertake activities that will give them a leg up on their college applications. In many cases, students from affluent areas seek advice from private tutors and counselors. These individuals open new networks and resources beneficial to students. Such is not the case for the students considered here.

Mushutu and Lily perhaps showed the greatest evidence of being involved in networks, but consider how these networks functioned. For the most part, Mushutu created his networks. He stitched together a non-stop focus on gaining acceptance to college and when he met a roadblock he moved on to another network. If one college preparation program seemed to be a waste of time or was ineffectual, he dropped that network and inquired about other possibilities. The after-school activities, clubs, summer programs, and weekend courses were voluntary associations he found on his own without any encouragement from teachers, families, or friends. Lily was almost the stereotypical class leader; she was popular with her friends, involved in class government, participated in planning the ever-popular homecoming and commencement, and consequently had preexisting networks that individuals in her position assumed from year to year (although none of the networks focused on college). Both of these students fared well because of their involvement in networks, but only Lily appeared to have a natural network that she did not need to demonstrate fortitude and aptitude in developing.

Our point here is that not every student ought to be assumed to have the personal determination of a Mushutu or the charismatic personality of a Lily. Those of us who care about the outcomes of the students who attend low-income schools need to help these schools develop a college-going culture. Such a culture begins with a sense that networking students in a college-going framework is essential. Networks need to be longitudinal, systematic, and able to withstand changes of teachers and students. Students frequently do not even know that it is in their best interest to join such networks. Rather than be seen as passive associations that students may join if they so desire, they need to be promoted as groups that actively seek and desire membership. Students without networks need to be made aware of possible associations that will help them, and networks need to be developed that incorporate and affirm individuals. If the goal is to increase college-going, then the solitary life that Juan led in school needs to be confronted by those who have access to the levers of change.

THE IMPORTANCE OF PEERS

Related to the importance of networks is the role of peers in going to college. All of these students, with the exception of Juan, were regularly in honors or Advanced Placement classes with students who were similar in academic skills and dispositions. Conversations about college and how to navigate the process were more likely to happen with these students than with individuals who attended other classes. However, the students were not in one big clique; they may have known of one another as would any senior in a similarly sized high school, but they were not all friends. At Commencement the principal pointed out that of the 577 graduates 68 were going to attend a four-year institution. He did not note that the attrition rate from ninth grade to twelfth grade is close to 70%. In the AP classes these students took, only 50% would take the exams, and less than 15% of the students would actually pass. Thus, even though these students were ostensibly the best in their institution, the culture of college-going was dramatically different from that of their peers in upper-income schools. In such schools, when someone enters an AP class the assumption is that he or she will be afforded the support and instruction necessary to ensure passing the exam.

Consider, for example, a comparable private high school located in a wealthy Los Angeles neighborhood. Over 95% of the students who start in the high school graduate and close to 98% of them go on to a four-year institution. A similarly high percentage of advanced placement students will take the exam and over 90% of the students will pass the exam with a score of three or above.

Students exist in peer groups. One need not be a scholar or psychologist to know that the individuals with whom students associate matter a great deal. However, very little thought has been given to fostering in peers a concern for attending college or what one must do to get into college. We entirely understand and concur with the concern about teacher quality and how to improve teacher education. We also readily acknowledge that how students learn in the classroom is fundamentally important, and that a home life geared toward helping students learn is essential. However, during the course of a day, week, or a student's high school career, the greatest amount of time an adolescent will spend is not with teachers or parents but with peers. The affiliations and associations students develop with one another have the potential to play a significant role in providing information and developing a culture where going to college is not just an abstract objective for some but a concrete goal for all.

A focus on peer groups and a concern for building a college-going culture in peer groups suggests that rather than a laissez-faire attitude where students associate with whomever they desire in whatever fashion they like, more deliberation ought to be given to how to direct relationships in a manner that accelerates discussions about college and what one needs to go to college. Visits to college campuses, for example, were relatively rare with these students. Jenny had visited some campuses, as had Trinity. Lily, Mushutu, and Juan, however, were not in peer groups where the possibility of visiting a college was actually discussed. Students had but a dim awareness about the difference between an Advanced Placement course and other classes so the motivation to take an exam was lost on them. Similarly, Jenny, Lily, and Mushutu were frequent visitors to the college center in school, but they did so as individuals more than as an activity they did with their friends. Deadlines came and went that the students frequently missed.

Peers need to be acknowledged as a social fact—they exist whether adults create them or not. The extent to which schools are able to focus peer groups in explicit manners and advance a college-going agenda provides one strategy about how to increase access to college.

THE RECOGNITION OF THE ROLE OF FAMILIES

Research on the role of parents and families with regard to their children's educational well-being has tended to swing wildly between a rejection of parents as knowledgeable caregivers and a romanticization of all parents as having the potential to play a central role in their children's decisions about going to college. What we found was a middle ground. Some parents, such as Jenny's and Lily's, played a central role in their children's decision to go to college. They made sure they did their homework, inquired about the colleges to which they were going to apply, helped them with their applications, and shared in the excitement when their children were admitted. They went to informational nights at school, had a sense of who their teachers were, and what they needed to do to get into college—even when they did not themselves have college experience, and even when they did not understand all the intricacies of applications and financial aid.

Mushutu's and Trinity's parents played different roles. Although Mushutu and Trinity clearly loved their parents and went to them for advice on a variety of matters, discussions about college happened elsewhere. Whether Mushutu applied to Stanford or Berkeley was a decision he made irrespective of what his parents had to say. He was not rebelling against them; he simply acknowledged that some people had better information on which to make a decision about college than his parents. Juan, too, loved his mother but he did not have conversations about college or education with her. Juan's father, however, played a negative role in his life. He did not even attend his son's high school graduation.

Two common concerns of all parents pertained to financial aid and the worth of college. None of these students or their families could afford to pay for college. However, other than the clear awareness of unaffordability, no one had a solid understanding about how to navigate the difficult terrain of financial aid. "Scholarship" was an unclear term that most understood as a synonym for a way to pay for college. Their parents uniformly did not even consider the possibility of taking out college loans, and did not understand the differences between federal, state, and institutional grants and scholarships. For some parents, although they supported their son's or daughter's desire to go to college, the overriding concern was how to pay for it. When I first spoke with Mushutu's parents, for example, his father asked if I would be able to find a college that would pay for his son's education. Lily's mom worried about debts; Jenny's parents did not understand the differences between public and private schools and their relative costs.

Not all parents were equally enthusiastic about their children going to college. Juan's father, and to a certain extent his mother, thought a job might be preferable. In part, the desire for a job was because it was tangible; their son would go off to work in the morning and come home with a paycheck, however paltry. A college day, especially a community college day, seemed odd. Juan slept late, took three buses to a college, and then spent the day reading in the library and taking classes at night. He obviously never returned with a paycheck from college. Lily had older siblings who went to college so her parents understood the value of a college education but were still concerned about their daughter attending college so far away. For Mushutu's parents, education was their top priority for their son, even though they were not able to help him in the formal application process.

Our conclusion after having watched these students as well as their friends and parents is that it is in no one's interest to assume an either-or approach with parental roles in education and college-going. In a perfect world one might reach out to all people and try to work with them in ways that enable them to mobilize their own and their community resources. Perfect worlds might house perfect parents, caregivers, and peer groups. These students live in no such perfect world. The pressures of earning an adequate income, immigration status, and single parenthood create challenges that make participation in school children's school lives very difficult. Rather than assume that educational policies need to reach all parents, and all parents need to play the same role, we are suggesting that, although adolescents definitely need adult advice and support en route to college that advice need not always come from the parent.

Clearly, some but not all parents can play a role in helping their children get to college. It is foolhardy to assume that every parent is able to fulfill that role; some parents are bystanders or even negative influences. Some parents are better equipped to help their children in other activities. In both instances the clear message is that when coupled with the knowledge that most children cannot navigate the college-going process alone, the system has to have support structures in place. Simply stated, to assert that *all* parents have to be supportive and knowledgeable about what their children need to do to get into college is to doom a substantial portion of children to inadequate support.

At the same time, many parents are able to play a role, and they will benefit from systematic, structured information. Too often, these parents were not equipped with information in a timely manner. Thus, they were able to lend their moral and emotional support to their children, but they could have done more to assist in preparing for college if they had been provided the necessary information and skills. We noted above, for example, that financial aid was a major concern to parents, but the information and seminars that included parents were confusing and given in a helter-skelter manner. Web sites and the Internet may be useful for parents who have a personal computer at home and at work, but they are of marginal utility for parents who are not computer literate. Letters and seminars conducted in English are less than satisfactory for parents whose primary language is Spanish.

It might be useful to think of college as a foreign land, first-generation students and their parents as the potential tourists, and those of us in the educational system as travel agents. For individuals who have traveled a great deal and the trip is to a country where the culture and language are the same as their country of origin, minimal preparation is necessary. For individuals who have not traveled abroad and the cultural distance will be significant, a great deal of preparation will be necessary. Frequently, novice travelers will not even know the right questions to ask other than, "Can we afford the trip?" When one looks back at the stories presented here, however, about how parents and their offspring received information about applying to college, one can only conclude that the travel agents were not very interested in advising and arranging a trip for these tourists.

THE REAFFIRMATION OF COUNSELING'S ROLE

If a particular entity does not exist, or is rare, then no one should be surprised if individuals do not use it. Thus, the fact that students do not make much of counseling is simply stating the obvious. Counseling in high schools is at a crossroads. Whereas private school students often have a phalanx of academic counselors and college counselors to advise them and their parents, in the schools we study there is generally one college counselor for the entire school. The college counseling office frequently doubles as a career center. A student who wishes to see the college counselor may have to wait months before being summoned by the counselor. Students' assigned guidance counselors focus on registering students for classes, supervision, and discipline, or preparing school reports mandated by state and federal laws and seldom have the time to discuss college plans with their charges.

Overcrowding has led to overlapping sessions where a certain segment of students are always off-track. Although such a schedule still enables students to take regular classes and graduate on time, it also creates a scheduling nightmare for counselors. Some students are off-track precisely at the time when college applications are due; other students are off-track when they should be signing up to take the SAT. Messages to students that are time-sensitive may or may not reach their destination because the students have no reason to come to school, email access is in short supply at school and home, and correspondence from school to home is less than optimal.

Our simple point here is that college counseling is in disarray. In the previous section we noted that not all parents are likely to play a central role in their children's decisions about going to college. If counselors are in short supply, overextended, and not very available to those students who are off-track, and some parents are either uninformed or unable to play a role, then does that suggest that teachers must pick up the slack?

Some, but not all, of these students had formed quite strong relationships with a teacher. Recall how Lily was moved by Mr. Holmby's nomination for a social studies award. Trinity also spoke highly of Mr. Holmby as her favorite teacher. Jenny relied on Ms. Jimenez for academic and emotional support. Juan, however, slipped through high school without ever finding a teacher on whom he could rely. Mushutu liked various teachers but no one stood out for him. Indeed, all of the students appeared to like and respect various teachers, but no teacher played a critical role in the decision processes utilized by the students about where to apply to college and how to get there.

Teachers, for their part, were generally consumed by their daily responsibilities. They saw their roles, logically, as teaching their charges the subject matter of the course. The vast majority of teachers we came across appeared well-informed, hard-working, and dedicated to their profession and their students. Many of the teachers also put in more hours than required and the students appreciated them. Mushutu's science teacher also doubled as the Academic Decathlon coach and had his students meet on Saturdays; he received no compensation for his work. One of the teachers held extra sessions over the holidays to keep his students motivated. Other teachers chaperoned at dances and proms, participated in homecoming and commencement activities, and arrived early at school and left late because they wanted to work with one or another student.

However, none of these teachers provided the students with whom we worked any systematic information about college-going. Yes, at times a teacher recommended a particular institution, or the AP teachers worked with students on how to answer questions on the exam. The month before applications were due students frequently had their English or history teachers take a glance at their essays and offer advice. Some AP English teachers even spent a class or two going over what should be on an essay.

Going to college is not a singular event, or a series of disjointed decisions and activities. The students with whom we worked were highly motivated and engaged. For the most part, the information they received about college was piecemeal and solicited through their efforts, not by concentrated actions on the part of teachers and counselors. On the one hand, public schools in the neighborhoods where we visited do not have a counseling staff that can handle the needs of even the best students such as those we interviewed, much less students who are average or below average. On the other hand, teachers are consumed by what they are paid to do—teach high school curricula. To foist even more responsibilities on high school teachers is a flawed strategy. To assume that teachers have the time and knowledge to adequately walk students through the various decisions one needs to make about college is foolhardy. Financial aid, for example, is a confusing jumble of regulations and processes that change from year to year. Although it is certainly possible that some teachers might be able to learn about financial aid and incorporate it into their lesson plans, we are not interested in the exceptional teacher who has particular knowledge and interest about financial aid. Rather, educational reforms need to be comprehensive so that they are not aimed at the extraordinary few, but instead are geared at overhauling the system.

A school that has one college counselor cannot convincingly claim that its goal is to get students into four-year institutions. Schools work on retention rates, graduation rates, and pass rates on exams. In the era of "No Child Left Behind," such statistical benchmarking is tied to state and federal accountability, definitions of quality, and funding opportunities. Although these are certainly related to who goes to college, the fact is that these are indirect effects. The schools we have visited and the ones where our students attended do not see as part of their responsibility getting students into college. By making such a point we are not laying blame at the schoolhouse door, or suggesting that an exposé be written about uncaring teachers or counselors—to the contrary. The cultural biographies we offer here are littered with positive examples of caring adults and ambitious students. Why, then, is the system failing to improve access to colleges and universities?

CONFRONTING THE SOCIAL ECOLOGY OF SCHOOLS

The last time Mushutu took his SAT exams we had made a bet. If he got under 1480 he had to take me out for a meal; if he got over 1480, I would take him to a restaurant. He sent me an email after he found out his scores at 3 A.M. "Dear Prof. I just checked my SAT scores. Amazing! I am just thrilled and excited. I got 770 on the math and 740 on the english. I broke the 1500. I guess you will have to take me to a dinner! Should I tell Stanford?"

My initial response after receiving Mushutu's email was enormous pride for him. Here was a kid with great gifts that he had applied with zeal and fortitude. He had succeeded despite numerous roadblocks that had been put in his way. He had the makings of yet another American success story. After I calmed down, however, a series of nagging feelings remained. I was troubled that he still had problems with his writing. I worried that he was not sure whether or how to convey the news of his test scores to Stanford. I wondered if a youth as gifted as he was still faced such formidable challenges, what did it suggest for those without his resourcefulness and abilities? Consider a message from Juan in response to a question about if we might get together one weekday night:

"Hello Sir," wrote Juan. "I'm doing ok. Yes, I free for a movie on Thursday. I not seen either movie you mention. I'm happy to go to either. School is ok. I am doing ok in English but the maths is difficult. Perhaps I get a job and still take classes at night. What do you think? I'm seeing you at 730 on Thursday, Sir."

This book has been a paradox. We have presented the cultural biographies of individuals in order to demonstrate how against remarkable odds high school students are able to succeed. Our intent has neither been to romanticize their lives nor to enshrine them as heroes. Nevertheless, each student in his or her own way worked as hard as possible and started out on the path for adulthood. Even as we wrote their stories, we struggled with our own instincts to think these students exceptional and their celebrations heroic. Despite our best efforts, the phrase "against the odds" rings in our heads and seeps into these pages. So we write the cultural biographies of exceptional students while also suggesting that their circumstances are not so exceptional.

The paradox does not end with the students themselves. The social ecology of the neighborhood in which these students grow up circumscribes a world fraught with trouble. By no means are we suggesting that these students come from a dysfunctional culture or that their backgrounds need to be disowned in order for them to succeed. In fact, we continue to be impressed with the resources available to these youths. However, the economic and social contexts in which these students are embedded present daunting challenges, even for those who are as gifted as Mushutu. The never-ending paradox in a capitalist democracy is that individuals have the ability to affect change that will improve their lives while at the same time they are caught in a net that all too frequently constrains choice and dampens the will to succeed.

In a democracy, society constructs the schools the citizens' desire. In the nineteenth century, America adopted compulsory education in large part because the citizenry accepted the idea that children needed to be educated about what it meant to live in a democracy and to be a citizen. An educated citizen, as defined by first a grade school and then a high school education, implied that the individual would be able to have a better job and be a better citizen than without an education. The passage of the Morrill Land Grant

Act suggested that higher education should be provided not only to the wealthy and religious, but also to those who were from the working class or poor. Public higher education throughout the twentieth century held tuition low because the citizenry accepted the state's obligation of paying for education. The implicit contract for these and other such actions was that the state assumed the lion's share of fiscal responsibility for education and the individual beneficiary agreed to work hard in school. The assumption was that when he or she graduated from school, democracy would be better off tomorrow than it was today. A well-educated citizenry implied an economically vibrant and healthy democratic public sphere.

To be sure, just as we do not wish to romanticize these students, we also do not wish to romanticize the American past. The educational system always has favored the wealthy over the poor. Far too often education for citizenship has meant the simple-minded and often pernicious assimilation of students of color to Anglo mores. Working class youths were more often than not trained for working-class jobs, and the wealthy assumed an entitlement to attend America's best universities. Nevertheless, the underlying ethos of acts such as compulsory education, public higher education, the false deflation of college tuition, and the like was that all individuals deserved an equal chance to succeed and contribute in a democracy. That ethos, however flawed, however imperfect, is now in danger of simply being abandoned.

Recall the facts of the neighborhood and school: Of 100 students who enter the high school where these students attended, less than five will end up going on to a four-year institution. In the Advanced Placement classes that are offered in that school, of the 50% of the students will take the final exam, less than 15% of the test-takers will pass the exam. The college office has one counselor. Sixteen percent of the teachers operate with an emergency credential. The school operates year round because of overcrowding and is open well into the night because it doubles as an adult learning center and community center. The average SAT score in the school is 830.

One hundred percent of students qualify for financial aid provided they meet citizenship or residency requirements. Home ownership in the neighborhood is approximately 5%. Less than 17% of adults in the neighborhood have a college degree; roughly 60% were born in foreign countries. There are three times as many check cashing storefronts as banks. Single-parent families are 23% of the local population.

The portrayal in the media of schools such as those where these students attended is often that of gang-infested buildings with metal detectors and police at every entrance. The schools are purportedly unsafe, and there is more than a hint that the vast majority of students are simply awaiting a lifetime of crime once they get out of high school. Such portraits are presumably in keeping with the statistics outlined in the paragraphs above. Further, the easy interpretation of such a portrait is that a culture of poverty breeds failure. A conservative response would be that any individual who tries hard can succeed and that simply throwing money at a problem will solve nothing. A neoliberal interpretation would be that if their cultural deficits can be overcome then of course these students can succeed.

Any painting and story probably has some strain of truth to it. Although we virtually always felt safe in the schools we visited and found the schools to be friendly and warm environments, we also locked our cars when we made a visit. We agree that simply throwing money at a problem will not solve an intransigent educational problem. We agree that all youth have the potential of succeeding if they are given a fair shake; indeed, part of what we take from these cultural biographies is the determination of individuals to succeed.

Where we disagree, however, is the lazy assumption that what simply needs to change is the individual—that if a student works hard or overcomes a particular character flaw then everything will be all right. We certainly concur with the initial points made in this chapter. Creating a more systematic framework for peer support and networking will improve a student's chances of going to college. Until decisions are made as to what structures should be put in place to counsel students effectively about going to college, there will be little dramatic change. If parents are educated about how to become more involved in helping their children get into college, then college attendance will increase.

However, what undermines individual improvement is an economic structure that places students such as Lily, Trinity, and Jenny at a distinct disadvantage. Yes, some students will succeed. Yes, if changes are made, more students are likely to succeed. Yes, if parents are involved then their children are more likely to be helped. What these stories point out, however, is the chronic problems that poor youths face in a society where a commitment to public education is on the wane. From the day they enter high school until the day they graduate, they are placed at a disadvantage when compared to their wealthier peers across town.

When the school board president stated at graduation that "sí, se puede" is not just a slogan but a way of life, he pointed out not only that we must believe we can, but that education is a communal undertaking—yes, *we* can. Educational policies aimed at individual improvement are useful and necessary. Individual struggles such as evidenced from the biographies of the students presented here are imperative. Ultimately, however, the challenge lies not in the frequently lonely, often heroic struggle of an individual to gain entrance to college, but in the communal commitment that provides the material, economic, social, and cultural support to extraordinary individuals such as Lily, Trinity, Mushutu, Jenny, and Juan.

• • •   • • •   • • •   • • •

Julia E. Colyar

A fterword

THE SYNTAX OF CULTURAL BIOGRAPHY

• • •

During the academic year 2003–2004, Jenny Acevedo was a senior in high school. She played soccer and volleyball, volunteered at her local church, and was involved in a college preparation program. She applied to several colleges and was admitted to each. These individual details of Jenny's experience, however, do not add up to a complete understanding of her path to college. As was the case with Lily, Trinity, Juan, and Mushutu, the details of Jenny's experiences are framed within a specific context, which is itself embedded within a larger social context. Understanding college-going for these students requires more than an attention to detail. At the same time, these details are where an investigation must begin.

The methodology used in this text was necessarily bifocal as we worked toward understanding the specific frames of student lives as well as the details that emerged from within. We attempted to capture the individual and the cultural contexts, as well as the individual within the cultural contexts— Jenny's experiences in a college preparation program, her home environment, and the community of Laurel City; Mushutu's movement between worlds and words; the ways in which Lily's path to college was marked by specific pages and larger concerns. Our bifocalism is evident in the methodological term we use to describe the chapters of this book: cultural biography. While we explored the personal elements of a life, we also looked beyond to the surrounding cultures. In representing the students' experiences, the two are dynamically intertwined.

The purpose of this afterword is to define and describe cultural biography as it was used in this text. Cultural biography, like qualitative research more generally, is as much "process" as "product." These pages are intended to address both. To that end, the first section provides a definition of cultural biography. In particular, the section presents the general characteristics and discusses our unique approach to the research process. The second section outlines the theoretical frameworks that inform the method. The specific activities in which we were engaged follow in the next section. The final section addresses the challenges of the writing process, and the afterword concludes with some thoughts about the promises of cultural biography as a policy tool.

TOWARD A DEFINITION OF CULTURAL BIOGRAPHY

"Cultural biography" has been used to describe texts for several generations, at least as far back as Henry Adams's *The Education of Henry Adams* (1946). Many volumes have recently appeared with the terms directly in the titles: *Anna of Denmark, Queen of England: A Cultural Biography* (Barrol, 2001), *The First Woman in the Republic: A Cultural Biography of Lydia Maria Child* (Karcher, 1998), *Walt Whitman's America: A Cultural Biography* (Reynolds, 1995), *Baroness Elsa: Gender, Dada and Everyday Modernity: A Cultural Biography* (Gammel, 2002), to name only a few. In each of these cases, the authors explore the contexts surrounding the central figures as a means of further understanding the individuals themselves. Put simply, the goals of such works are to articulate the relationship between social and personal lives. In David Reynolds's 1995 biography of Walt Whitman, for example, the poet's experiences are contextualized within the divisive politics of the Civil War and the American literary and artistic renaissance.

Gelya Frank's *Venus on Wheels* (2000) provides a more intentional definition of cultural biography, including the researcher as intimately connected to the "culture" represented in the final product. Unlike the authors in the recent cultural biographies listed above, Frank's context overlaps with her participant's; Gelya Frank and Diane DeVries are not separated by time and history. Frank can literally dialogue with her participant about the particular context in which they are both enmeshed. Writing about Walt Whitman one hundred years after the poet's death, Reynolds does not have the luxury of this dialogue, or even firsthand experience in the nineteenth century. "Culture," in texts like Reynolds's, has a quality of stasis: Culture of the nineteenth century has elsewhere been recorded and made manageable. Reynolds enlightens both Whitman and the American context as he superimposes the two, but ultimately the biographer does not inscribe aspects of culture. In other words, Frank's cultural biography constructs "culture" in ways Reynolds's cannot.

The approach to cultural biography in this text acknowledges the dia-logic opportunities of contemporaneous research and writing—we under-stand our roles in co-constructing culture just as we reflect existing cultural values. While we do not replicate Frank's model in this text, the processes and ideas are important as she details the ways in which "culture" is con-structed. Her definition will be discussed at some length here.

In her book, Frank describes the life of Diane DeVries, a woman born without arms or legs, while also examining the cultures of femininity and dis-ability. She defines cultural biography as a "cultural analysis focusing on bio-graphical subjects that makes use of ethnographic methods, along with life history and life story, that critically reflects on its methodology in action as a source of primary data, including the effects of power and personal factors" (2000, p. 22). Further, Frank notes the importance of cultural milieu in the research process; individuals—researchers and participants alike—are shaped by social systems, but they also serve as primary actors in that system. She describes data as recorded from observations and interviews, the stock-in-trade of qualitative work. A second layer of data comes from the researcher's experience of listening and responding to the participant. The researcher acts as a mediator between the participant and the biography; the "culture" inves-tigated in Frank's text is not simply the contemporary context in which DeVries and Frank are situated, but also the set of images Frank herself uses to categorize and organize the biography. Frank defines her role as "a proxy for future readers" (p. 23); she gauges her interpretations and responses, examining and re-examining them as they are situated in social contexts. The set of relationships Frank describes in this process are complex and overlap-ping—the researcher, the participant, and the social context are engaged in a kind of group handshake. In this way, Frank makes explicit the role of the researcher in the meaning-making process.

Ultimately, Frank describes the finished cultural biography as comprised of "images" interpreted and represented by the researcher. Such images are important, as are the processes by which these images come to the fore. While some qualitative methodologies downplay the importance of the researcher's reflexive interpretation (Frank, 2000), Frank's cultural biogra-phy takes advantage of it. Cultural biography, Frank asserts, "considers how specific biographical images arise and goes on to interpret them in terms of cultural processes" (p. 22). The distinctions here are subtle but essential: Frank is working not only with cultural norms, values, and processes—abstractions that are not always codified into discrete "things"—but also with "images." In many cases, the images in Frank's text are photographs or other media reproductions, but they are also images constructed in the researcher's (and later the reader's) mind. These images are culturally defined; they serve as organizational systems that help individuals make sense of their own or another's thoughts and actions. Of necessity, Frank's presence in the text, as writer, actor, and image-constructor, is substantial. In order to understand the images Frank records and analyzes, a reader must also "see" her in the research process.

In this text, the question of the researcher's role is also important. As interviewers, observers, and interpreters, the authors were present at every step. Indeed, the complex relationships we negotiated between data, participants, and ourselves reflect larger postmodern interests in subjects and social theory (Denzin, 1986). The "crisis of representation" that haunts qualitative work still hovers: As I sat down in front of a computer screen, I inevitably asked: "How can individuals be represented in written texts? Whose story is told, and by whom?" I am reminded of the uncertainty that guides much of qualitative work, and of the questions of power and voice necessarily at the heart of such inquiries. Frank's definition of cultural biography provides an important place for us to begin addressing these questions as they relate to the students in these chapters. For Frank, stories told are personal and cultural; they reflect individual values as well as broader social imagery. Power resides in participants and the researcher, but of equal strength in her work is the power inherent in images.

Rather than situate ourselves as proxies in the reading of these students' lives, however, we chose to take one step back from the represented pages. Our presence is clear—it cannot be otherwise—but our goal was not to negotiate meanings as primary characters in the story. Frank's analysis emerges from her dialogues with DeVries—the text literally depends on Frank's voice and exchanges with her participant. Our presence is important in these chapters because we ultimately recorded the stories, but the significance of these narratives did not depend on our presence. Rather, we set these individual narratives in motion, aware that the various plots reflected our influence and resonate with readers' experiences, memories, and expectations. The "images" we wrote toward and against were those of "college preparation" and "college-going." What these pages present are unlike the images most often associated with young people preparing to move into postsecondary settings.

Frank's definition of cultural biography is helpful in that it gives vocabulary to our goals: We wrote about college preparation focusing on biographical subjects; we relied on ethnographic methods, including life history and life story strategies; we recognized that our participants were culturally situated and we sought to articulate the relationship between individual and social lives; we reflected on this methodology itself as a source of data, particularly as we negotiated the role of the researcher in constructing and reflecting student cultures.

We also recognized the ways in which this project differed from Frank's definition. Three additional characteristics are useful in clarifying our approach to cultural biographies: a focus on youths, the process of collaborative ethnography, and connections to policy.

YOUTHS

Cultural biography, like many qualitative approaches, relies on an attention to individual lives. Biographical accounts often provide more opportunities for understanding lives than typically found in quantitative work. "Cases," Miller (2000) notes, can attain an identity that statistical analysis "must deny them" (p. 8). Inherent in the definition of biographical accounts is age and experience; a discussion of critical stages and processes is difficult when the participant has "nothing" to report. Many well known life histories reflect the tendency for researchers to work with adult participants: Brown's *Mama Lola* (1991), Lewis's *The Children of Sanchez* (1961), Behar's *Translated Woman* (1993), and Burgos-Debray's *I, Rigoberta Menchú* (1983) each report the retrospective events of a life from the vantage point of adulthood. While we do not dispute the importance of experienced perspectives, we also believe that biographical accounts of younger participants can be similarly rich in detail, reflective, and complex.

The slices of life scrutinized by researchers and young participants are necessarily defined with different senses of time. Rather than looking across a number of years, this project aims at recording more contained experiences. For example, in these biographies, moments in line at a café, 50 minutes of a class period, or an afternoon at home with a headache provide significant data points. "Time" in these cases changes meaning as we focus on the college-going process, which has specific parameters and deadlines.

This approach also acknowledges the roles of young adults in navigating the college process and the larger social spheres. Rather than viewing these students as passive players in the system, reported about by experienced adults, we place their narratives, experiences, and ideas at the center of our investigation. As these pages attest, these young people are highly motivated, committed to their educations, families, and cultural histories, and deeply thoughtful as they make sense of and relate their experiences.

COLLABORATIVE ETHNOGRAPHY

This project is also unique in that it brings together researchers, students, and school contexts. Historically, biographical projects have been individual exercises which use the "Lone Ranger" approach (Douglas, 1976): Individual researchers "single-handedly" pursue data, process findings, and present understandings. In this project, we take a different path, one which benefits from individual commitment and collective processing. Though each of the cultural biographies in this text reflect the work of a single researcher and student(s), the findings discussed in the conclusion are collective. In this way, our process borrows from collaborative ethnographic projects.

In recent years, collaborative or "team" ethnography has been used as an innovative means of approaching a variety of social phenomenon (May & Pattillo-McCoy, 2000). As May and Pattillo-McCoy define it, collaborative ethnographies are "those studies in which two or more ethnographers coordinate their fieldwork efforts to gather data from a single setting" or a single "social phenomenon" (2000, p. 66). The goal of the approach is in expanding and improving the ways researchers collect data, process findings, and present their work (May & Pattillo-McCoy, 2000; Gerstl-Pepin & Gunzenhauser, 2002; Woods, Boyle, Jeffrey, & Troman, 2000). For May and Pattillo-McCoy, the particular methodologies of collaborative ethnography share the means of individual ethnography, but individual researchers then "compare" and integrate field experiences. As a result of comparing and discussing, ethnographers "highlight more than one perspective of the complex social world" and "highlight" the various angles of an "ever-changing set of social phenomena" (p. 67). This process not only juxtaposes observations and brings various findings to the table, but it also provides an opportunity for the researchers to explore their own subjectivities in the process. For example, in this work, we often met to discuss the events at the school sites and the experiences of various students, but we also talked at length about our roles as researchers, recorders, and writers. Our personal experiences were an explicit part of our conversations as we worked toward understanding the students' lives. Ultimately, our research and writing was enriched by the opportunity to discuss our findings with one another and place these students into a larger context.

As will be discussed in the description of our methodology below, each researcher was responsible for independently working with individual students. Our collective focus was aimed at the intersection of a "single setting" and a "social phenomenon:" as a team, we explored the college-going process for five students enrolled in their junior or senior years of high school. Though not strictly a "single setting" as some of the students were enrolled at different schools, the settings were singular in that they were situated in urban, low-income areas with high proportions of minority student enrollment.

POLICY CONNECTIONS

As with qualitative work generally, we do not suggest that the findings from cultural biographies like this project are generalizable; the strengths of biographical methods are in nuanced understandings of specific things, people, and cultures, not in sweeping statements about successful college preparation. First and foremost, findings from this study help us understand the complexities of *these* students' lives, not all students' lives. At the same time, however, we believe that fine-grained inquiry and analysis bring life to our understandings of students, families, schools, and communities, and can enlighten the details oftentimes glossed over in survey research.

Our goals in this project, then, include those of cultural biography in general, but we also seek connections to policy and policy-making. Frank describes cultural biography as a means to provoke and inform cultural analysis. While we value this definition, we work toward translating these biographies into policy recommendations that can circle back into communities, school systems, and college preparation programs. We believe this process has much to add to current understandings of educational processes and next steps in research, policy, and practice.

FRAMEWORKS: NARRATIVE AND EMPLOTMENT

As suggested earlier, cultural biography joins the chorus of qualitative research that responds to the "crisis" of postmodernism. From postmodern theory generally, cultural biography starts with the notion that experience is individual and cannot be represented using traditional tools of research—traditional tools too often reflect modern, rational systems. Instead of claims of authority, postmodernism argues in favor of perspective and relativist positions, multiplicity, fragmentation, and the empowerment of "the other"—a variety of subjugated communities, groups, and ideas (Bloland, 1995; Rosenau, 1992).

As postmodernism calls for new images and understandings of self and society, one of the central tools in this process is language and narrative construction. Theorists such as Jean-François Lyotard imagined the postmodern project as a search for new narratives and perspectives, a language system outside of the "grand narratives" of Modern philosophy (1984). As Denzin (1986) notes, "the texts of culture can no longer be read as 'realist' extensions of actual experiences" (p. 195). Rather, "culture" is seen as a "semiotic, linguistic production"—culture is assembled by a variety of narratives. Denzin's "production" is an important term in this definition; it suggests the ways narratives act as building blocks for larger social values and systems. In addition, "production" anticipates the concept of "emplotment," the act of constructing characters within particular environments. Emplotment is a purposive activity wherein characters are described within relationships, contexts, and situations; these relationships and contexts appear as scenery but also help define individuals and their worlds. Cultural biography relies on the narrative construction of lives and the process of emplotment. From constructed tellings, truths come into view: Truths emerge in the narratives participants articulate about their lives, the narratives that underlie the research dynamic, and the narratives that mirror and reflect social contexts (Frank, 2000). Because of the centrality of narrative and emplotment in this methodology, these two concepts are further outlined in the next section.

NARRATIVE AND VOICE

Like qualitative research generally and cultural biography particularly, "narrative" can be defined as *product* and *process*. In terms of product, narratives are data points a researcher collects, disassembles, reassembles, and retells (Hones, 1998). In order to be "collected," narratives must also be discrete units, definable as with particular structures and forms. Perhaps the simplest means of defining narrative is via plot and sequence: Narratives are linguistic units with clear beginning, middles, and ends (Labov, 1982). The process of narratives is more complex. Polkinghorne (1988) defines narrative as "a meaning structure that organizes events and human actions into a whole" (p. 18). Here, Polkinghorne echoes Lyotard's definition, which looks beyond representational "objects" to practices of "customary knowledge" (Lyotard, 1984, p. 19). In this definition, narratives are the means by which individuals understand the world. Narrative provides a structural framework—a sense of plot and passage of time—which can be used to order experience. Narrating, then, is an act of meaning-making; in order to narrate an experience, we must first process, re-order, and in some way resolve the experience. We also understand another's stories through these same linguistic processes we use to order and make coherent the stories of our own lives (Polkinghorne, 1988).

This definition of narratives closely echoes the ways in which Frank uses "images" in her definition of cultural biography. Frank (2000) argues that experience is organized into meaningful information by processing the images that experience creates. Again, these images arise from cultural practices and constructs; the images Frank works with are not only those from external sources, but also those the researcher has in mind. In this text, we acknowledge the importance of images, but also step back further to narratives, which are embedded in images themselves. In this way, we again attempted to distance ourselves—albeit only insofar as the researcher is able to remain separate—from the texts and data that students brought to our research project.

Jenny Acevedo, for example, narrated about school and home life as we sat together at Starbucks. "Sometimes," she started, "when I do my homework really late, and I'm like so tired, Tony will come in and sit on the floor next to me, and it's just so great. [The kids] give me energy to stay awake and finish my homework." The narrative is short and discrete; Jenny's story started with a general sense of time ("sometimes") and continued until she finished her homework. The process of meaning-making in this case occurred as Jenny recalled, ordered and articulated these details. Though it is reasonable to expect that Jenny "saw" her brothers as she narrated this scene, the imagery was not explicitly part of the data. As cultural biographers we then used individual narratives like these to construct a larger text.

Lyotard highlights individual narratives like Jenny's in his work rather than asserting a single or "grand" narrative. His argument is for a diversity of voices and authorities, where "grand" or metanarratives are replaced by unstable and interactive exchanges, as well as individual voices articulating distinct experiences. As Jenny and I talked, for example, our communications were always negotiated and situational. Such negotiation and situation are essential for understanding complex social activities, and they are essential for disabling traditional power dynamics (Quantz & O'Connor, 1988). In this way, Jenny, Lily, Trinity, Juan, and Mushutu were participants in the research rather than a "subject" to be scrutinized. The students' voices were important in the formation of new understandings. Individually, and collectively in their diversity, these students' narratives had authority because of their individuality and distinction.

For Lyotard, the notion of voice also points to questions of power and empowerment (1984). He argues that narratives carry their own authority rather than speaking to a larger system. Establishing legitimacy for Jenny's narrative did not come from external authority; her narratives have "truth" and "meaning" because she chose to articulate them. Only with such an expansive definition of what counts as "meaningful" can the power structures of the modern world be upended and contested.

Implicit in this discussion of narratives is the concept of voice and culture. Voice, the utterance itself, acts as an agent in social exchange. If narratives are imagined as a means of organizing and presenting information, voice is the tool that underlies narrative performance. Quite literally, voice is the vehicle of narrative expression. "Voice" is also a term researchers use metaphorically to denote agency. When narratives are individually authorized and valued, voices are also authorized and valued. And as voices shape narratives and social discourse, they also shape culture (Quantz & O'Connor,

1988). Tanaka (2002) takes this notion even further, arguing that "having voice means having culture" (p. 266). His point is well taken: As scholars look to diversify our understandings, it is not enough to "settle" for having diverse voices included as add-ons (p. 267). Tanaka argues for research that applies "voice" broadly as a means to "validate many different cultures in education" (p. 267). Voice thus expresses the shared meanings of a culture that derives from race, ethnicity, gender, sexual orientation, class, immigration status, physical capabilities, and combinations therein (Tanaka, 2002).

Somers (1994) points out that this definition takes more traditional notions of narrative as representation and reappropriates it as an ontological process. Through narrativity, she notes, "we come to know, understand, and make sense of the social world," as well as "constitute our social identities" (p. 606). "All of us come to be *who* we *are* (however ephemeral, multiple, and changing) by being located or locating ourselves (usually unconsciously) in social narratives rarely of *our own making*" (p. 606; original emphasis). Such narratives came from history, from collected experience translated into stories (p. 614). Here, Somers points back to Lyotard's questions of power and narrative; Somers makes the point that "grand narratives" often shape who we are as they shape social narratives. Her argument for the ontological nature of narratives—the ways narratives help form identities—again reiterate the potential for individual stories in meaning-making. However, our approach was not to rely on the unconscious processes that Somers alludes to; these unconscious processes are akin to Lyotard's grand narratives. Rather, we assumed that the process of narrative was empowering precisely because voices can shape identities outside of these larger constructs.

EMPLOTMENT

Cultural biography is a method that brings together individual experiences and the social systems in which they are framed. Narratives serve as primary tools in this process; narratives communicate particular events, and they reflect broader cultural themes and practices. One of the central characteristics of narrative is emplotment: "Narratives," Somers explains (1994), "are constellations of *relationships* (connected parts) embedded in *time and space,* constituted by *causal emplotment*" (p. 616; original emphasis). Somers continues:

> Unlike the attempt to produce meaning by placing an event in a specified category, narrativity demands that we discern the meaning of any single event only in temporal and spatial relationship to other events. Indeed, the chief characteristic of narrative is that it renders understanding only by *connecting* (however unstably) *parts* to a constructed *configuration* or a *social network* of relationships

(however incoherent or unrealizable) composed of symbolic, institutional, and material practices. (p. 616; original emphasis)

Somers's definition is useful because it makes clear the importance of context; narratives themselves, as discrete units, cannot be fully understood. Narratives always refer to—are in some ways constituted by—connections to social networks. Rather than "specified categories" of meaning—what Lyotard again might term "grand narratives"—narratives convey meaning via the emplotment that places them in connection with other systems, other plots and circumstances. Emplotment "gives significance to independent instances" and provides "historicity and relationality" (Somers, 1994, pp. 616–617). Plot, says Somers, is the "logic or syntax of narrative" (p. 617).

This discussion is also useful as Somers complicates the notion of "plot." Narratives must have plot and temporality; being able to discern when one narrative begins and ends makes it possible to collect narratives as data. "Plot" thus refers to some sequence of events; how these events are arranged depends on the speaker and their individual practices. Practically speaking, plot can be imagined as the skeleton of a narrative. Plot provides the structure around which further details can be secured. For example, the plot of the short narrative included above was even shorter: "Jenny's brother sat in her room while she did homework." Without the clarity provided by plot, the narrative would be difficult to recognize and process. However, plot alone does not convey the complete meaning in Jenny's narrative. Missing from this skeletal plot is Jenny's sense of family, academic responsibilities, and personal determination. These details are available because of the surrounding narrative, and because of the additional narratives that make up the larger chapter. A second level of emplotment came when we gathered these chapters together. Meanings emerged because of dynamics within the narratives as well as across these chapters and lives.

Somers (1994) brings up another important element of plot discussions. As she describes the ontological aspects of narrative, she also argues against a strictly representational definition of narrative. Like Polkinghorne and Lyotard, Somers reminds us that plot and, by extension, narrative, are processes. Plots are not static representations but interactive systems. Plots and narratives are expressive and reflective of identities; they help define who we are, leading to discoveries about what we do. Such a definition of plots and emplotment helps mediate against non-theoretical misunderstandings of representations (Somers, 1994, p. 617). Narratives are not simply individual or personal "stories." They are significant expressions of personal experience and the complex environments in which they are constructed.

Emplotment, then, is a characteristic of narrative production at the level of the speaker, but it is also a characteristic of the cultural biography process.

Our aim with these chapters is to present individual students without removing them from their neighborhoods, communities, schools, and other social networks. We present these young adults as emplotted characters—the social constellation is always present and always reflected in their individual stories.

BRINGING THE METHOD TOGETHER

Before moving on to the specifics of data gathering and writing, it is useful to review the plot of cultural biography. Simply stated, cultural biography is a methodological approach that superimposes individual narratives and social systems. Our research is near- and farsighted; both perspectives are important in understanding how these students make progress through high school and into college. Rather than investigating students' experiences in a decontextualized manner, our research seeks to understand individual biographies and cultural systems as interacting in ways that enhance what we know about each. The story that gets articulated, then, is one of culture and the individual. This process is important as it enlightens what we know about student experiences, foregrounding individual experiences in favor of stereotypes and generalities. Moreover, it is important as a means of allowing diverse voices to enter the larger conversations about class, race, and college preparation.

ACTORS AND ACTION: THE RESEARCH PROCESS

This text derived from a larger study of college preparation programs for low-income youths, and from more than a decade of research on the topic. We have been interested in state-sponsored programs, privately funded scholarships and mentoring activities, financial aid challenges and celebrations, and after-school activities that support youths in their educational endeavors. We worked with a variety of programs, and in these contexts, we also interacted with a diverse group of students: Latino/a, African American, Asian American, and students from mixed backgrounds. Students came from urban and suburban communities, and they represented the spectrum of economic levels. Our work emphasized the cultural components so often missing in college preparation activities, and we wrote about the importance of supporting students from within their specific contexts rather than through programs aimed at majority students.

Over the course of two years, the research team, funded by a Department of Education grant, looked at a variety of programs in California and examined the ways in which their efforts affect college-going outcomes. We were interested in student plots and narratives, but also in the constellation of influences around individual students: families, culture, peers, academic coursework, co-curricular activities, mentors, and high school counselors. An examination of college preparation, we believed, must include specific details and cultural contexts. Following extensive case studies of the programs themselves, the project turned to individual students. The final phase of the project included producing cultural biographies for a select number of high school juniors and seniors; Jenny, Lily, Trinity, Juan, and Mushutu were invited to participate.

STUDENTS

All of the students in this project expressed a previous interest in attending college, and most were participants in college preparation programs available through their specific high schools. Each was identified and contacted by the individual researcher. In most cases, students were recommended by college prep program advisors and teachers. In other words, the student participants did not represent a random sample. We were particular in our selection. For example, I met with a college prep advisor and asked for recommendations: "Who has participated in the college prep program and can talk about his or her experience? Who might be interested in talking with me? Who can commit to the time required in this project—weekly meetings with a researcher?" Based on the advisor's suggestions, I talked with Jenny Acevedo in one of the hallways of the main office; she was enthusiastic about participating, her eyes bright as she nodded in response to my initial questions. We agreed to meet two weeks later for our first formal interview.

Like Jenny, all of the students included in this volume were looking toward college, though some had clearer visions than others. Their "level" of preparation—test scores, academic record, or knowledge about particular colleges—was not part of our selection process. In some cases, we met with students for several months without knowing exact facts and figures from their transcripts. Rather, we chose students with the following common characteristics: a member of a minority group, first generation college-goers, enrolled in urban schools, and from low-income families. We did not choose students for this project based on the assumption that they would go to college; rather, we chose students with some aspiration, and we worked with students who also chose to work with us. We were fortunate to have been introduced to such interesting and interested research partners. Their commitment was substantial: We met with each student weekly over the course of 12 months.

RESEARCHERS

As a research team, we began this process with an interest in educational equity generally, college preparation particularly, and individual students most narrowly. We were each, and still are, students of educational policy and this methodological approach. Some of us approached the research table with years of experience in faculty positions, some with experiences as high school and elementary school teachers, and others with experiences working with college students. We came from a variety of disciplinary fields as well as cultural backgrounds.

Throughout the data collection and writing, our individual skills and interests were enhanced by the opportunity to work together. The members of the research team share office space, making communication and discussion an almost daily activity. More formal discussions were scheduled monthly. During these meetings, the team talked about preliminary findings and made plans for the continuing project.

Team meetings were also important opportunities for reflection about our research positions and interactions with the students. Our engagement with Jenny, Juan, Mushutu, Trinity, and Lily went far beyond traditional relationships between interview participants. We did not attempt to maintain a professional distance with our students; rather, we sought to develop trusting relationships and a sense of shared goals. These distinctions are difficult to articulate, but it is important to point them out. In working with these students, we sought to engage them in ways that would provide a sense of ownership in the process and its outcomes. Unlike Gelya Frank and her work with Diana DeVries, we did not seek friendships with these students. Instead, we acted as trusted adults in these young people's lives. In our many casual conversations, the students turned to us for mentorship and advice about college applications, financial aid, and homework problems.

DATA COLLECTION

Quite similar to life history, cultural biography relies on a variety of data collection techniques (Frank, 2000). Although we, the researchers in this project, approached our work independently, much of our activities overlapped. As we learned more about the individual students, we sought additional information; we worked together to strategize new resources and opportunities for further understanding. Our data collection is therefore only mostly uniform—because we worked with different students and families, we used different specific activities. Connecting our work was the overarching goal of understanding students, their individual contexts, and the larger world of college preparation.

The central research technique used in this study was interviews. Over the course of a year, each of us interviewed our students weekly. These meetings generally lasted one to two hours, and often longer. Though some interviews were conducted over the telephone, the majority were conducted in person: at the high schools, at a local Starbucks, at various restaurants, at the students' homes. These interviews were taped and transcribed, and we maintained detailed field note journals. In addition, we interviewed many individuals associated with our particular students, including parents, siblings, and friends. The research team also spent a great deal of time interviewing at the school sites. We talked with teachers, principals, guidance counselors, and other students. In particular, we met frequently with the staff in the college guidance office; a member of the research team visited the office weekly.

Formal and informal observations were also important in this study. In the guidance office and all around campus, we spent at least two hours per week observing campus activities. Formally, we observed student committee meetings, club gatherings, and assemblies. That is, we introduced ourselves as observers and conspicuously noted the happenings and dynamics. Perhaps our most formal observations were in classrooms: We filed through hallways and into classrooms, and we listened in while teachers discussed Spanish poetry, Shakespeare, physical science, American history, and much more. Each of us spent two full days attending classes with our students, and we often met during lunch or after school.

Many of our observations were informal. In schools as large as Esperanza, the presence of another adult is mostly unremarkable, and extracurricular activities were important opportunities to gather data about school culture. In the fall, we attended the high school homecoming game and watched the varsity football team lose to a cross-town rival. Some of us attended the junior prom in the spring—"A Magical Night." We also toured the school buildings with our students; Lily pointed out the place where kids go to smoke, and Trinity warned against one of the breezeways that connected the various building sections. "Gangs," she said. Sitting in the courtyard during the brief lunch period, we observed student interactions and watched the movement of various cliques around tables. As these pages suggest, sometimes we were mistaken for school officials, and sometimes we were assumed to be high school students ourselves.

Outside the walls of the high school, we shopped with our students, attended community meetings and family celebrations, stood on street corners observing the goings-on of the neighborhood, or watched the process of a haircut in a local salon. We attended financial aid and college workshops offered by community groups, and toured college campuses with our students; we attended end-of-the-year awards ceremonies and graduation.

Between scheduled interviews and observations, we often corresponded with students via email or telephone. These exchanges were also important sources of data, sometimes providing information we otherwise didn't know. In practical terms, email correspondence helped us schedule meetings with students who were in class all day and unavailable by phone. In these chapters, we have included some of these email messages. We have retained the original text without correcting for grammar or spelling in an effort to bring the students' unique electronic voices to the page.

BACKGROUND INFORMATION

Throughout this volume, we included specific information about the community surrounding Esperanza High School, the secondary school many of our students attended. These data are invaluable in understanding the student narratives; our conversations did not take place against a plain green backdrop the way movies are lately filmed—the background separate, even computer generated, filled in after the fact to fit particular scenarios. The Esperanza community backdrop is rich in data, and these details are part of the students and their narratives. Because they are not necessarily explicitly addressed in our interviews, we sought out and present them here as connective tissue in these chapters. Information about community demographics, economics, and housing trends are in every narrative; we sought to bring them to this book as well.

Background information was collected through school demographic data, community fact sheets, and government census information. We reviewed many school documents in search of data, including accreditation reports and newspaper articles. While waiting in the counseling office for interviews, we reviewed school and community documents. We read the school paper, looked at the school Web site, and reviewed the "report card" required by state mandate of every public school. Perhaps the simplest way to describe all of these methodological efforts is to note that we spent time getting to know our students, their families, their school contexts, and their communities. All of these experiences contributed to our understandings.

Our interviews, observations, and document analyses were also completed with an eye toward policy—as suggested in our definition of cultural biography, we were concerned with extending our discussions into policy circles. The most important goals of our time with the students were to understand more about their individual and community lives, to be sure. While we observed, asked questions, and made plans for future meetings, however, we also had policy questions in the backs of our minds. Policy questions were not articulated directly to students or parents—what secondary school structures provide sustained support for college access? How do decision-making processes in college admissions offices reflect the diversity of student experiences and talents? However, as we talked with students and processed our experiences individually and collaboratively, our thoughts were directed by such questions.

The research both concludes and restarts with the writing process. In the next section, I describe the process of writing these individual cultural biographies.

THE WRITING PROCESS: COMPLETE SENTENCES TOWARD A COMPLEX PROCESS

These chapters began with five pages. Like all writing projects, of course, the "beginnings" were relative; we began the writing process as a means of analyzing the data we had collected. At the time, we had not completed all of our data collection. We did not know what the final product would look like, how many pages it would fill, or how we could possibly organize the wealth of data into a coherent and complete chapter. Would we "start" our chapters with first interviews? The first activities of the research grant? The moment when our students ceased being a "research participant" and waved at us from across a crowded hallway with the familiarity of a co-conspirator? Because these questions are unanswerable at the start of such a process, we began with five pages—our first attempt at putting complete sentences toward a complex process.

Our first five pages naturally varied by author: For example, my pages were organized thematically, while the pages of another team member were organized chronologically. We did not write with the expectation that these pages would constitute the first words of our completed chapter. If we did not know before starting, we quickly learned that we would write multiple drafts, using multiple organizing principles. Indeed, in most cases, these first five pages have all but disappeared from our texts entirely; those pages are still present, as they are relevant to our experiences of research and our descriptions of our students. However, their shapes have changed.

We used the writing process as one means of analyzing our experiences and the narratives students related to us; we also used these initial writing activities as a means of looking ahead to the possibilities of our final texts— we used the writing to plan future drafts as we struggled over how to represent our participants. Writing and thinking are inextricably intertwined; with so many pages of field notes, transcriptions, and pictures in our minds, we wrote to think through our research questions as well as the findings that were slowly gathering around us. As we came to know the students better, our texts became more complex; writing a discrete chapter became more difficult and much easier. In many ways, writing these cultural biographies was itself an ontological process; we continuously worked toward understanding the research and our own writing.

Cultural biography is also a collaborative process. Because each member of the research team was engaged in the difficult process of putting complete sentences to a complex task, peer editing was important—our analyses of the biographies we were crafting were enhanced by our conversations, and our writing was strengthened as we exchanged drafts. Each of the students represented in these pages have also reviewed their chapters for accuracy, veracity, and feel. Their trust and commitment to the project could only be met with reciprocal trust and commitment on our parts; as the students trusted us to record their experiences, we trusted them to provide feedback on the manuscripts. We used the students' feedback to temper our subjectivity and positionality. None of the research team attended Esperanza High School; we do not share the same socioeconomic backgrounds and experiences. Juan, Mushutu, Lily, Trinity, and Jenny are perhaps the most important readers of these chapters. They alone can spot the missing details, gestures, or bits of conversation that can change how we understand the narratives that make up this text.

THE ARTS AND SCIENCES OF CULTURAL BIOGRAPHY

Our presentation of students' lives was intentional. Given the difficulties of the process as suggested above, and given the great variety of interviews, observations and field notes, we sought a means of representing these stories in ways that acknowledged complexity but appealed to simplicity. Thus, we presented these chapters in moments and events rather than in grand portraits. While this effort was practical—how to deal with so many data?—it was also aimed at stylistic innovation. Rinehart (1998) writes about the increasing need for sociological and ethnographic writing that reaches beyond the ordinary to forms more convincing, compelling, and experimental. "Clearly," Rinehart explains, "there is a sense of lyricism and even of magic in lived experience that is outside the ken of quantitative social 'science' discourse: by reducing experience to its component parts, some of this magic . . . is lost" (p. 201). Qualitative research has also been accused of being too scientific, un-engaging, and unlyrical (Denzin, 1997; Richardson, 1997). By working toward more artistic presentations and representations, Rinehart argues that ethnography can "better answer differing questions" (p. 201).

Rinehart also notes that life experiences do not happen in discrete, manageable units. Experience "comes at a rush," without linear organization and often in fragmented parts. As experiences are emplotted—as individuals reform experience into narratives—meaning, sense, and categories can be assigned. Indeed, this project began with a framework that acknowledged the power of narrative ways of knowing. Individual experience may be fractured, but emplotment allows for arranging and a means of connecting to communities and institutions.

These cultural biographies reflect the sometimes disorder of experience in the manner we present them. We shaped these texts in an effort to write more compellingly and convincingly; we ordered the details of student experiences in particular ways for the purpose of communication and feeling. Denzin (1997) articulates the importance of "feel": "Seeing is not understanding. Understanding is more than visual knowledge. Understanding is visceral" (p. 46). For Rinehart, this visceral quality is not developed in the weight of overwhelming detail. Description that is believable and holistic may include mere glimpses—glances that are more emphatic than overt reports. Rinehart continues:

> What is enough detail, and what is too much detail is one of the fundamental differences between believable and cloying, between engaging and pedantic, between creatively accurate and merely replicable and boring writing. In this sense, then (as in life itself), the empty spaces, or the silences, serve to verify the existence of the telling detail just as surely as does the detail itself. The spaces serve as markers of connection, lyrical markers of writing that is fundamentally magic. (p. 206)

In these pages, we recorded the many details of student lives. We described classrooms, family conflicts, and the contents of students' backpacks. We presented these details knowing they were specific sites from which to begin our research, and knowing they were elements of larger cultural and social systems. We also presented them knowing they do not add up to a complete understanding of college preparation. We understood that college-going, like the syntax of cultural biography, cannot be completely mapped. We left some of the spaces of these biographies empty—we knew they served as places of opportunity, celebration, and continued study.

One of the consequences of the presentation style we used was a renewed understanding of power relationships and positions. As Rinehart discusses, attention to the writing process itself can make us better, more reflective researchers, which in turn can improve quality of our writing. Further, understanding the process of qualitative writing, including cultural biography, is an important step in understanding "how stories, with all their embedded craft and art, may oppose, or reify, or slightly skew the existing power relationships" (p. 202). Such reflection is important for all research acts, but it is particularly poignant in projects that seek to raise the voices of individuals often muted by position and circumstance. Writing cultural biographies was instructive in querying the problem of college access, but not simply because the questions were clearer and the challenges more easily recognized. The research and writing process brought us into dialogue with students and their cultural settings, and we had to negotiate the unequal power relationships inherent in the research act. Of particular importance, however, was the circumstance that we, the researchers, were actors in the system to which these students aspired. This fact made us more unequal partners while at the same time making us better situated to provide assistance when needed. Such a complex dynamic was not easily expressed in words and sentences, but the challenge of empowering students while also inhabiting powerful positions certainly influenced our research and representations.

FROM BIOGRAPHIES TO POLICIES

While the goals of cultural biography include understanding student experiences within social spaces, the finished chapters we presented here are not complete knowledge, the last words in the problem of college access. We cannot expect to answer all questions about inequitable educational attainment for low-income, urban minority youths in these pages, nor do we assume any methodology could. College preparation is not solvable in the same ways equations are solvable. However, we are hopeful about cultural biography's potential in exploring difficult questions and understanding vexing problems. Solutions, in any form or completeness, cannot be achieved without an accurate and thoughtful understanding of the problem itself. Ultimately, we offer these cultural biographies as springboards for rethinking educational policy regarding access to college and resources for minority high school students.

As difficult as the writing process was, the translation into policy will undoubtedly be even more complex. Our writing compressed the individual and the social surroundings into words on a page; we now offer these biographies back to social spaces so that they can be unfolded and examined with different lenses. Undoubtedly, some will be suspicious of these findings for all the usual reasons: These biographies are specific, not generalizable, incomplete in revealing information about a community or type. We argue, however, that we sought deep knowledge about individual students so that strategies can be developed based on details rather than assumptions; we presented these students as emplotted characters so that educational practices can better respond to the complexities of student lives; we sought individual voices and narratives so that the stereotypes about urban high school students could be disrupted. Educational policies, including policies that respond to equity and diversity, were established before the current undergraduates were even in elementary school—indeed, long before researchers had even an incomplete understanding of what "diversity" means. These cultural biographies are presented to fill in the silences of what we do not yet understand, and to press forward to more complete policy, practice, research, and understanding.

Epilogue

...

The young men and women introduced in these chapters are still on our minds as this text goes to press. After these last words, there are still pages yet to be written for Mushutu, Juan, Jenny, Lily, and Trinity. New challenges and opportunities are waiting.

Mushutu is a freshman at Stanford University; he intends to double major in electrical engineering and international relations.

Juan is working and taking courses at a community college. He is still struggling academically.

When Jenny enrolled at the University of California at Berkeley, she decided to return to using her given name, Yeni. She is now in her second year at UC Berkeley, where she is studying political science, ethnic studies, and Chicano studies. Yeni still dances Salsa and plays soccer.

Lily is in her second year at the University of California at Santa Cruz, where she is considering double-majoring in feminist studies and psychology with an emphasis in history. She is passionate about dance, and she is a co-founder of Centroamericanos Unidos (a Central American students' club).

Trinity is completing her second year at the University of California at Santa Barbara. She joined the Residence Life Government Board as a freshman, and has decided to major in pharmacology. She still wants to go to UCLA, but is now looking forward to matriculating as a graduate student.

References

...

Adams, H. (1946). *The education of Henry Adams.* Boston: Houghton Mifflin.

Barrol, L. (2001). *Anna of Denmark, Queen of England: A cultural biography.* Philadelphia: The University of Pennsylvania Press.

Behar, R. (1993). *Translated woman.* Boston: Beacon.

Bloland, H. (1995). Postmodernism and higher education. *Journal of Higher Education, 66*(5), 521–559.

Brown, K. (1991). *Mama Lola: A Voudou priestess in Brooklyn.* Berkeley: University of California Press.

Burgos-Debray, E. (1983). *I, Rigoberta Menchú.* (A. Wright, Trans.). London: Verso.

Cook, T. D., & Payne, M. R. (2002). Objecting to the objections to using random assignment in educational research. In F. Mosteller & R. Boruch (Eds.), *Evidence matters: Randomized trials in education research* (pp. 150–176). Washington, DC: Brookings Institution Press.

Denzin, N. (1986). Postmodern social theory. *Sociological Theory, 4*(2), 194–204.

Denzin, N. (1997). *Interpretive ethnography: Ethnographic practices for the 21ˢᵗ century.* Thousand Oaks, CA: Sage Publications.

Douglas, J. D. (1976). *Investigative social research: Individual and team field research.* Beverly Hills, CA: Sage.

Frank, G. (2000). *Venus on wheels.* Berkeley: University of California Press.

Gammel, I. (2002). *Baroness Elsa: Gender, Dada and everyday modernity: A cultural biography.* Cambridge, MA: MIT Press.

Gerstl-Pepin, C., & Gunzehauser, M. (2002). Collaborative team ethnography and the paradoxes of interpretation. *Qualitative Studies in Education, 15*(2), 137–154.

Hones, D. (1998). Known in part: The transformational power of narrative inquiry. *Qualitative Inquiry, 4*(2), 225–248.

Howe, K. R. (2004). A critique of experimentalism. *Qualitative Inquiry, 10* (1), 42–61.

Karcher, C. (1998). *The first woman in the republic: A cultural biography of Lydia Maria Child.* Durham, NC: Duke University Press.

Labov, W. (1982). Speech actions and reactions in personal narrative. In D. Tannen (Ed.), *Analyzing discourse: Text and talk* (pp. 12–44). Washington, DC: Georgetown University Press.

Lewis, O. (1961). *The children of Sanchez.* New York: Vintage.

Lincoln, Y. S., & Cannella, G. S. (2004). Dangerous discourses: Methodological conservatism and governmental regimes of truth. *Qualitative Inquiry, 10*(1), 5–14.

Lyotard, J. (1984). *The postmodern condition.* (G. Bennington & B. Massumi, Trans.). Minneapolis: University of Minnesota Press.

Maxwell, J. A. (2004). Causal explanation, qualitative research, and scientific inquiry in education. *Educational researcher, 33*(2), 3–11.

May, R.A.B., & Pattillo-McCoy, M. (2000). Do you see what I see? Examining a collaborative ethnography. *Qualitative Inquiry, 6*(1), 65–87.

Miller, R.L. (2000). *Researching life stories and family histories.* London: Sage Publications.

Mosteller, F., & Boruch, R. (2002). *Evidence matters: Randomized trials in education research.* Washington, DC: Brookings Institution Press.

Polkinghorne, D. (1988). *Narrative knowing in and the human sciences.* Albany: State University of New York Press.

Quantz, R.A., & O'Connor, T.W. (1988). Writing critical ethnography: Dialogue, multivoicedness, and carnival in cultural texts. *Educational Theory, 38*(1), 95–109.

Reynolds, D. (1995). *Walt Whitman's America: A cultural biography.* New York: Knopf.

Richardson, L. (1997). *Fields of play: Constructing an academic life.* New Brunswick, NJ: Rutgers University Press.

Rinehart, R. (1998). Fictional methods in ethnography: Believability, specks of glass, and Chekhov. *Qualitative Inquiry, 4*(2), 200–224.

Rist, R. C. (2000). Influencing the policy process without qualitative reason. In N. K. Denzin & Y. S. Lincoln (Eds.), *Handbook of qualitative research* (2nd ed.) (pp.1001–1017). Thousand Oaks, CA: Sage.

Roseneau, P.M. (1992). *Post-modernism and the social sciences.* Princeton, NJ: Princeton University Press.

Shavelson, R.J., & Towne, L. (2002). *Scientific research in education.* Washington, DC: National Academy Press.

Somers, M.R. (1994). The narrative constitution of identity: A relational and network approach. *Theory and Society, 23*(5), 605–649.

Tanaka, G. (2002). Higher education's self-reflexive turn: Toward an intercultural theory of student development. *Journal of Higher Education, 73*(2), 263–296.

Whitehurst, G. (2003, April). *The institute of education sciences: New wine, new bottles.* Paper presented at the annual meeting of the American Educational Research Association, Chicago, IL.

Woods, P., Boyle, M., Jeffrey, B., & Troman, G. (2000). A research team in ethnography. *Qualitative Studies in Education, 13*(1), 85–98.

Yin, R.K. (1984). *Case study research: Design and methods.* Beverly Hills, CA: Sage Publications.

Contributors

...

Julia E. Colyar is an assistant professor of Educational Administration and Higher Education at Southern Illinois University, Carbondale, where she teaches courses in student affairs administration and qualitative research methods. She previously worked as an academic advisor for undergraduate students, and has taught undergraduate courses in writing and literature. Her research focuses on access and transitions to college for underrepresented students, learning communities, and classroom discourses.

Zoë Blumberg Corwin, a former high school Spanish teacher, is a research assistant at the Center for Higher Education Policy Analysis at the University of Southern California. Corwin is pursuing a doctorate in sociology with an emphasis in race, gender, and education. Her dissertation focuses on college transitions for youth in foster care. Along with Drs. Tierney and Colyar, Corwin is the co-editor of *Preparing for College: Nine Elements of Effective Outreach,* a book exploring the most useful components of college preparation programs.

Paz M. Olivérez is a James Irvine Foundation fellow and research assistant in the Center for Higher Education Policy Analysis. She is currently a Ph.D. student studying Educational Policy and Administration at University of Southern California and holds a B.A. in Sociology from the University of California, Santa Cruz. She previously worked as a kindergarten teacher and substitute teacher for middle and high school. Her research interests include the high school to college transition of low-income students of color, with a focus on the college access and financial aid issues of undocumented immigrant students.

William G. Tierney is Wilbur-Kieffer Professor of Higher Education and Director of the Center for Higher Education Policy Analysis at the University of Southern California. He has received funding from the Ford, Irvine, Lumina, and Pew Foundations to pursue research pertaining to access and equity in the academy. In addition to access-related research, his scholarship investigates academic freedom, faculty work, and organizational reform.

Kristan M. Venegas is an assistant professor of Higher Education at the University of Nevada, Reno. Her research interests include financial aid decision making for low-income students, college access, and qualitative research methods. She has received support for her work from the James Irvine Foundation and the Lumina Foundation and was a research assistant in the Center for Higher Education Policy Analysis at the University of Southern California.

Index

...

Questions about the
Purpose(s) of Colleges
and Universities

Norm Denzin,
Joe L. Kincheloe,
Shirley R. Steinberg
General Editors

What are the purposes of higher education? When undergraduates "declare their majors," they agree to enter into a world defined by the parameters of a particular academic discourse—a discipline. But who decides those parameters? How do they come about? What are the discussions and proposed outcomes of disciplined inquiry? What should an undergraduate know to be considered educated in a discipline? How does the disciplinary knowledge base inform its pedagogy? Why are there different disciplines? When has a discipline "run its course"? Where do new disciplines come from? Where do old ones go? How does a discipline produce its knowledge? What are the meanings and purposes of disciplinary research and teaching? What are the key questions of disciplined inquiry? What questions are taboo within a discipline? What can the disciplines learn from one another? What might they not want to learn and why?

Once we begin asking these kinds of questions, positionality becomes a key issue. One reason why there aren't many books on the meaning and purpose of higher education is that once such questions are opened for discussion, one's subjectivity becomes an issue with respect to the presumed objective stances of Western higher education. Academics don't have positions because positions are "biased," "subjective," "slanted," and therefore somehow invalid. So the first thing to do is to provide a sense—however broad and general—of what kinds of positionalities will inform the books and chapters on the above questions. Certainly the questions themselves, and any others we might ask, are already suggesting a particular "bent," but as the series takes shape, the authors we engage will no doubt have positions on these questions.

From the stance of interdisciplinary, multidisciplinary, or transdisciplinary practitioners, will the chapters and books we solicit solidify disciplinary discourses, or liquefy them? Depending on who is asked, interdisciplinary inquiry is either a polite collaboration among scholars firmly situated in their own particular discourses, or it is a blurring of the restrictive parameters that define the very notion of disciplinary discourse. So will the series have a stance on the meaning and purpose of interdisciplinary inquiry and teaching? This can possibly be finessed by attracting thinkers from disciplines that are already multidisciplinary, for example, the various kinds of "studies" programs (women's, Islamic, American, cultural, etc.), or the hybrid disciplines like ethnomusicology (musicology, folklore, anthropology). But by including people from these fields (areas? disciplines?) in our series, we are already taking a stand on disciplined inquiry. A question on the comprehensive exam for the Columbia University Ethnomusicology Program was to defend ethnomusicology as a "field" or a "discipline." One's answer determined one's future, at least to the extent that the gatekeepers had a say in such matters. So, in the end, what we are proposing will no doubt involve political struggles.

For additional information about this series or for the submission of manuscripts, please contact Joe L. Kincheloe, joe.kincheloe@mcgill.ca. To order other books in this series, please contact our Customer Service Department at: (800) 770-LANG (within the U.S.), (212) 647-7706 (outside the U.S.), (212) 647-7707 FAX, or browse online by series at: www.peterlang.com.